Felice Giardini and Professional Music Culture in Mid-Eighteenth-Century London

Felice Giardini and Professional Music Culture in Mid-Eighteenth-Century London explores Giardini's influence on British musical life through his multifaceted career as performer, teacher, composer, concert promoter and opera impresario.

The crux of the study is a detailed account of Giardini's partnership with the music seller/publisher John Cox during the 1750s, presented using new biographical information which contextualizes their business dealings and subsequent disaccord. The resulting litigation, the details of which have only recently come to light, is explored here via a complex set of archival materials. The findings offer new information about the economics of professional music culture at the time, including detailed figures for performers' fees, the printing and binding of music scores, the charges arising from the administration of concerts and operas, the sale, hire and repair of various instruments and the cost of what today we would call intellectual property rights.

This is a fascinating study for musicologists and followers of Giardini, as well as for readers with an interest in classical music, social history and legal history.

Cheryll Duncan is Senior Lecturer in Music at the Royal Northern College of Music in Manchester, UK. Her primary research interests concern music culture in Britain during the late seventeenth and eighteenth centuries, with a particular focus on records of the equity and common-law courts. She has published articles in *Cambridge Opera Journal*, *Early Music*, *Journal of the American Musicological Society*, *Journal of the Society for Musicology in Ireland*, *Opera Journal*, and *Royal Musical Association Research Chronicle*, and has contributed a chapter to *Geminiani Studies*, ed. Christopher Hogwood.

Royal Musical Association Monographs
Series Editor: Simon P. Keefe

This series was originally supported by funds made available to the Royal Musical Association from the estate of Thurston Dart, former King Edward Professor of Music at the University of London. The editorial board is the Publications Committee of the Association.

No. 30: **The Genesis and Development of an English Organ Sonata (2016)**
Iain Quinn

No. 31: **The Regulation and Reform of Music Criticism in Nineteenth-Century England**
Paul Watt

No. 32: **Upper-Voice Structures and Compositional Process in the Ars Nova Motet**
Anna Zayaruznaya

No. 33: **The Cyclic Mass**
Anglo-Continental Exchange in the Fifteenth Century
James Cook

No. 34: **The Pre-History of The Midsummer Marriage Narratives and Speculations**
Narratives and Speculations
Roger Savage

No. 35: **Felice Giardini and Professional Music Culture in mid-eighteenth-century London**
Cheryll Duncan

For more information about this series, please visit: www.routledge.com/music/series/RMA

Felice Giardini and Professional Music Culture in Mid-Eighteenth-Century London

Cheryll Duncan

LONDON AND NEW YORK

First published 2020
by Routledge
2 Park Square, Milton Park, Abingdon, Oxon OX14 4RN

and by Routledge
52 Vanderbilt Avenue, New York, NY 10017

Routledge is an imprint of the Taylor & Francis Group, an informa business

First issued in paperback 2021

© 2020 Cheryll Duncan

The right of Cheryll Duncan to be identified as author of this work has been asserted by her in accordance with sections 77 and 78 of the Copyright, Designs and Patents Act 1988.

All rights reserved. No part of this book may be reprinted or reproduced or utilised in any form or by any electronic, mechanical, or other means, now known or hereafter invented, including photocopying and recording, or in any information storage or retrieval system, without permission in writing from the publishers.

Trademark notice: Product or corporate names may be trademarks or registered trademarks, and are used only for identification and explanation without intent to infringe.

British Library Cataloguing-in-Publication Data
A catalogue record for this book is available from the British Library

Library of Congress Cataloging-in-Publication Data
A catalog record has been requested for this book

ISBN: 978-0-367-32205-2 (hbk)
ISBN: 978-1-03-208804-4 (pbk)
ISBN: 978-0-429-31727-9 (ebk)

Typeset in Times
by Deanta Global Publishing Services, Chennai, India

Contents

List of Illustrations   vii
Acknowledgements   viii

Introduction   1

1 **The documents**   5
  Legal background 5
  Physical description 6
  Case summary and outcomes 7

2 **Biographies**   9
  Felice Giardini: early years in England 9
  John Cox: music trader and publisher 22

3 **Early collaborations**   33
  First publications 33
  Giardini's royal licence 38
  Subscription concerts 43
  Mr Ogle's series 1751–52 45
  Giardini/Vincent series 1753 50
  Giardini/Chabran series 1754 57
  Giardini/Frasi series 1755 60
  Giardini and the Opera 1756–57 63

4 **Giardini and Cox in court**   67
  Giardini's indebtedness to Cox 67
  The publication of Giardini's Overtures 69
  Cox's administration of concerts and operas 74

vi Contents

5 Giardini's account at Cox's music shop 77
Violin costs 78
Giardini's other instruments 80
Music purchases 82
Other expenses 88
Advertising costs 88
Giardini's picture 94

Conclusion 99
Appendix 1: Schedule A1 102
Appendix 2: Giardini's associates 109
Index 121

Illustrations

2.1 Felice Giardini and Violante Vestris – marriage allegation   19
2.2 Felice Giardini and Violante Vestris – marriage bond   20
2.3 Auction of John Cox's stock-in-trade   30
2.4 Robert Bremner's purchase of Cox's plates   31
3.1 Subscription proposals for Giardini's *Sei sonate* Op. 3   35
3.2 Advertisement for Giardini's *Sei sonate* Op. 3   37
3.3 Giardini, *Sei sonate a violino solo e basso* Op. 1   39
3.4 Cuthbert Ogle's licence for the Great Room, Dean Street, 1752   47
3.5 Advertisement for the Giardini/Chabran subscription series   58
5.1 Red ticket for Giardini's benefit concert in May 1753   91
5.2 Thomas Gainsborough, Portrait of Giardini (oil on canvas) *c.*1758. Knole House, Kent   95
A2.1 Pier Leone Ghezzi, 'Domenico con Suo Fratello Bresciani'   115
A2.2 Advertisement for personnel to emigrate to the Americas   116

Acknowledgements

I am indebted to the anonymous readers for their helpful and encouraging comments on the manuscript form of this monograph, to Simon Keefe and the production team at Routledge for their guidance and to Hugh Belsey, Martin Harlow, David Mateer and Michael Talbot who gave so freely of their time and expertise. I am also grateful to the Royal Northern College of Music for the period of study leave that enabled me to bring this project to fruition.

Introduction

Public musical life of the sort we recognize today first emerged in England during the eighteenth century. By about 1750 London was perhaps the most musical city in Europe, to judge from the volume and variety of its musical activity. Music lovers with sufficient wealth and social status could choose between a multiplicity of diversions to suit their taste and purse. The Italian opera, based at the King's Theatre in the Haymarket, was among the finest in Europe, and the large salaries it paid attracted the best singers and musicians of the day. Musical productions could also be enjoyed at the English playhouses in Covent Garden and Drury Lane, and nearly all plays were decorated with songs, dances and entr'acte music. In the summer the various wells, spas and pleasure gardens mounted ambitious musical programmes; at Vauxhall, for instance, one could hear pastoral songs, martial airs, concertos for wind or brass and dance music. London's concert scene, too, was rich and dynamic; public concerts not only began there but also became far more numerous and varied than anywhere else in Europe. In addition to events that anyone might attend by purchasing a ticket, concerts of a more private nature were organized by musical societies, fashionable soirées, early music groups and convivial glee clubs.

The musical life of eighteenth-century London took the vigorous form it did for a number of interconnected reasons. Critical to the growth of public performances during the period was the withdrawal of royal and direct aristocratic patronage, which led musicians to make their living independent of any one patron or institution; forced by economic necessity to broaden their horizons, they turned their attention away from the court to the affluent homes and public places of the metropolis. Other determinants were the growth in consumerism and the general commercialization of leisure in which music participated; 'by charging for admission, public concerts made of music a commodity offered to and demanded by a new

2 *Introduction*

breed of cultural consumers'.¹ Another important factor was the weakness of governmental controls on business and the printing press, which further encouraged musicians to seek out potential markets in the unexploited avenues of their profession; publishing and concert management thus became two more areas of contact between opportunists in the music industry and the world of business. The freelance musician now not only performed and composed but also taught regularly, sold or published music, ran music in theatres and promoted concerts. William Weber has summed up the situation succinctly: 'London's musical life accordingly grew out of entrepreneurship, rather than state or municipal authority of the sort central to musical life on the Continent'.²

By mid-century the foundations had been laid for the even greater expansion of concert-giving that coincided with the arrival in England of the composer and violinist Felice Giardini (Degiardino and variants). Two aspects of his musicianship account for the explosive impact he had on London audiences both at his début in April 1751 and subsequently. Giardini was no run-of-the-mill composer/violinist; he brought to the concert life of the capital an ingredient that had hitherto been lacking – a technical command of his instrument that one can only describe as virtuosity. He was also an exponent of the latest continental music, and the new repertoire that he introduced to élite consumers satisfied their thirst for novelty and made him the darling of the *beau monde*. Indeed, to paraphrase an authority on music in eighteenth-century England, the foundation of the modern symphony-concert series can effectively be traced back to 1751, for the two Giardini overtures performed at his London début were the British public's first exposure to Italian symphonies in the modern pre-Classical vein.³

William Weber could have been thinking specifically of Giardini and his early years in England when he penned the following general thoughts on musical opportunism, so pertinent are they to the composer's particular situation at the time:

> By definition, musical life tended to have a limited number of institutions and practices that were controlled by musicians established within them, and it was therefore incumbent on any outsider to seek

---

1   Catherine Harbor, 'The birth of the music business: public commercial concerts in London 1660–1750'. 2 vols. (Ph.D. dissertation, University of London, 2012), 1:304.
2   William Weber, 'London: A city of unrivalled riches', in *Man and music: The Classical Era from the 1740s to the end of the 18th century*, ed. Neal Zaslaw (London: Macmillan, 1989), 293–326, at 295.
3   Simon McVeigh, *Concert life in London from Mozart to Haydn* (Cambridge: Cambridge University Press, 1993), xiv.

out fresh opportunities. Indeed, the history of musical life amounts to a series of successful and unsuccessful entrepreneurial efforts to make an impact on established tastes and institutions. In order to succeed as a high-level professional, a musician had to acquire a broad set of social skills by which to identify and accomplish promising opportunities. It was insufficient just to be a good performer or composer; to rise to the top of the profession almost always required musicians to be able to find patrons, attract a public, lead other musicians, and indeed, organize productions of an often complicated order. That involved learning techniques of self-promotion through exposure in public and in print, through personal contacts and idiosyncratic personal behavior, and linking to all this a distinctive and appealing musical style.[4]

As a virtuoso Giardini was 'intrinsically an opportunist', and he quickly perceived and took advantage of the openings that presented themselves in London.[5] What follows is a study of the various manifestations of that entrepreneurial spirit as recorded in a host of archival and literary sources dating mostly from Giardini's first decade in England. These include newspapers, correspondence, memoirs, Charles Burney's literary remains, and local and governmental administrative records. However, special attention is paid to the wealth of documentation surrounding Giardini's drawn-out legal struggle with his business associate and – for want of a better word – manager John Cox. This litigation, which has only recently come to light, contains new information about the economics of professional music culture at the time, including detailed figures for performers' fees, charges arising from the administration of concerts and operas, and the cost of what today we would call intellectual property rights. Until now, specific sums for these aspects of the music business have been in very short supply.

Given the importance of the litigation involving Cox and Giardini, it is right that it should take centre stage; however, a certain amount of preliminary groundwork needs to be laid before a coherent picture can emerge. After a brief description and discussion of the legal sources, new biographical information about the main players is presented to help contextualize their business dealings and subsequent disaccord. Chapter 3 then relates some of the data gleaned from the litigation to Giardini's multifaceted career as composer, performer, concert promoter and opera impresario.

---

4 William Weber, 'The musician as entrepreneur and opportunist, 1700–1914' in *The musician as entrepreneur 1700–1914: Managers, charlatans, and idealists*, ed. William Weber (Bloomington: Indiana University Press, 2004), 3–24, at 5.
5 Weber, 'The musician as entrepreneur and opportunist, 1700–1914', 6.

A detailed look at the reasons for the break-down in his relationship with Cox follows, in which the latter's less than perfect printing of one of the composer's collections played a pivotal role. Finally, the account that Giardini held at Cox's music shop for the period 1751–58, a copy of which forms part of the legal record (see Appendix 1), is analysed to provide further insights into the diversity of his interests and the symbiotic nature of his association with Cox. Several entries record the costs he incurred in pursuit of various entrepreneurial activities, including those relating to concert management and advertising; teaching and performance; the purchase, printing and binding of music scores; and the sale, hire, modification and repair of various musical instruments. Not all of Giardini's business ventures were successful, and some ended in bitter recrimination and strife, but the influence he had on the artistic life of London in the second half of the eighteenth century was profound and lasting.

1 The documents

Legal background

The archives on which this monograph draws for much of its material consist of litigation generated by two disputes heard in different courts of the English judicial system. The first dates from Easter 1758 when John Cox brought suit against Felice Giardini; this was heard on the 'plea' side, that is, the civil – as opposed to the 'crown' or criminal – side of the Court of King's Bench, the highest common-law court in the land. The second case, preserved among the records on the equity branch of the Court of Exchequer, was instituted in the following term as a response by Giardini (now the complainant) to Cox's common-law action. The primary business of the Exchequer, of course, was to call the King's debtors to account; secondarily it was a court of law where cases affecting the rights and revenues of the Crown were heard and determined. The Exchequer Court had two sides – a common-law jurisdiction (the so-called 'Exchequer of Pleas') and an equity side. The word 'equity', which is synonymous with fairness and natural justice, was often used in contrast with the common law. Whereas the latter was the more confining, rigid and predictable system, equity was more flexible, discretionary and individualized. It helped to supplement the substantive common law and provided a broader array of remedies, such as specific performance, injunctions and accountings. The equity courts (Chancery and the equity side of the Exchequer) were regarded as courts of conscience, and bills of complaint were presented there to persuade the Lord Chancellor or the Exchequer Barons to relieve the petitioner from an alleged injustice that would result from a too rigorous application of the common law. Until the middle of the seventeenth century, litigants in the Exchequer had to have some genuine connection with the royal revenue, but from 1649 that connection persisted only as a legal fiction for most plaintiffs. Anyone claiming to be indebted to the Crown could sue another upon a writ of *quominus*, that is, of his being 'the less' able to satisfy the Crown

6   *The documents*

by reason of the cause of action he had against the defendant. This is why Giardini's Exchequer bill begins: '(1) ... Your Orator Felice Degiardino of Brewer Street in the parish of Saint James in the Liberty of Westminster *and* County of Middlesex[,] Italian Musick Master[,] Debtor and Accomptant to your Majesty'.[1]

Physical description

The proceedings in King's Bench comprise Cox's initial declaration expressing the wrong he has suffered at the hands of the defendant; a claim for damages; the record of several imparlances or adjournments subsequently granted by the Court to Giardini's attorney; and the setting of a trial date. This material is inscribed on the recto and verso of two strips of parchment or 'rotuli' measuring 65cm × 22.8cm and 65.7cm × 22.8cm, respectively, the standard size of rotulus for a King's Bench plea roll.[2] The documents that constitute Giardini's Exchequer case, by contrast, are more numerous and come in a variety of shapes and sizes.[3] Held together by a thong in the top left corner, they include:

Document 1: Giardini's bill of complaint, measuring 80.3cm × 86.2cm. The initial drafting is not dated, but it must have been presented to the Court sometime between 26 May and 14 June (Trinity term) 1758. According to a marginal note the bill was 'Amended by Order of Court made the 11th of December 1758', probably in light of Cox's testimony in Documents 2 and 4 below; there are a number of interlineations and marginalia as a result.

Document 2: Cox's answer, measuring 135.7cm × 83.2cm. Filed on 11 November 1758, this enormous document contains two Schedules (A1 and A2), the first of which is reproduced in a diplomatic transcription as Appendix 1 of this study. The word 'Schedule' in this context encompasses detailed accounts and lists attached by one party or another,

---

1   Editorial policy with regard to the transcription of extracts from the legal proceedings is as follows: line numbers, allowing the reader to locate quotations from the original documents, are provided in round brackets; interlineated text is shown between converging obliques (\ ..../); contractions and abbreviations are expanded in italics; superscript letters, capitals and original spelling have been retained; and editorial additions, including minimal punctuation, appear in square brackets.
2   The National Archives of Great Britain (henceforth TNA): KB 122/286 (Easter 31 Geo. II), rot. 478; word-count: 3113. Although there are two rotuli, only the first is numbered; this is quite usual, the number changing only with the next case on the plea roll.
3   TNA: E 112/1235/3444 (Trinity 31 Geo. II); word-count: 21,225.

usually the defendant, to their pleadings as evidence in support of their case.

Document 3: Giardini's exceptions, measuring 39.8cm × 25.5cm. An 'exception' was a formal objection by the complainant that the defendant's answer was insufficient or in error, specifying the grounds for that objection. This modest document was filed after Document 2, at some point during Michaelmas term 1758.

Document 4: Cox's further answer, measuring 70.2cm × 45.8cm. To satisfy the objections raised by Giardini in Document 3, Cox was required to testify again, and a marginal note tells us that this sworn statement was made 'at Serjeants Inn the 25th day of Nov$embe^r$ 1758 before Richar^d Adams'.

Document 5: Cox's answer to the amended bill, measuring 68.5cm × 63.3cm. Delivered on 6 February 1759, this includes two more Schedules (B1 and B2), which are reprinted in Chapter 4 and at the end of Chapter 3, respectively.

Document 6: Giardini's replication to Cox's answers, measuring 25.6cm × 16.4cm. A 'replication' is a second pleading of the complainant's case, in response to the defendant's answer. This dates from Hilary term 1760 and is purely formulaic.

Document 7: Cox's rejoinder to Giardini's replication, measuring 25.5cm × 16.3cm. A 'rejoinder' is a second pleading of the defendant's case. This is also dated Hilary 1760 and is of similarly low evidential value.

Case summary and outcomes

Before examining the documents in greater detail, it may be helpful to summarize the main points on which the parties were at variance. In broad brush-stroke terms, the litigation charts the rise and fall of the business relationship between a professional musician (Giardini) and his publisher, music seller and manager (Cox). As we have seen, it was the latter who initiated proceedings in King's Bench at Easter 1758; without defining the nature of his business, Cox complained that Giardini owed him several sums of money not only for unspecified goods and services, but also for cash loans. The composer countered almost immediately by resorting to equity in the hope of obtaining an injunction that would restrain Cox from pursuing his suit; the lengthy Exchequer proceedings that followed are invaluable because they flesh out the skeletal generalities that characterize not just this, but most, common-law actions. Giardini may have pinned all his hopes on equity, for he appears to have withdrawn gradually from the King's Bench case over the coming months. The trial that had been set for the end of Trinity term 1759 never took place and, in the Court's rules and orders

8 *The documents*

for the following Michaelmas, a marginal note to a case-list that includes Cox v. Giardini reads: 'Unless something be said in Arrest of Judgment on Saturday the tenth day of November let Judgment be entred [*sic*] for the Plaintiff'. Giardini's legal team did not comply with this order, knowing full well that the matter was under consideration in the Exchequer.[4] A series of injunctions issued there certainly impeded the progress of Cox's lawsuit but they did not quash it, and on Tuesday 17 June 1760 the Court threw out Giardini's complaint because he had failed to pursue it:

> Between Felice DeGiardino Pet*itioner* & John Cox Def*endan*t By Amended Bill
> Upon the Motion of Mr Bicknell the Younger of Councel for the Def*endan*t Informing the Court that the said Def*endan*t Obtained an Order of this Court in Hilary Term last for Dismissing the pl*aintiffs* Bill for want of prosecution after Answer filed[;] whereupon the pl*aintiff* Replyed but had Not proceeded Since[.] He therefore prayed that the said pl*aintiffs* Bill might stand Dismissed Out of this Court for want of prosecution with Costs to be taxed by the Dep*u*ty Rem*embrance*^{r} of the sa*i*^{d} Court[,] which the Court hereby Orders as prayed unless Cause be Shewn to the Contrary on the last Day of this Term[5]

Again Giardini did not respond, which is why we hear nothing further of his case.

The above extracts from the Courts' deliberations are worth quoting because they bring a sense of closure to the dispute, and leave us to ponder the state of Giardini's finances, which must have been parlous after payment of damages and costs. But the legal consequences are perhaps the least interesting aspect of the litigation from a musicological point of view. Of much greater significance is the wealth of fascinating detail concerning London's musical life during the 1750s that both parties adduce as evidence in the course of constructing their cases; this will be discussed mainly in Chapters 3–5.

---

4 TNA: KB 125/156 (Rule Book 1759–60).
5 TNA: E 127/41 (Order Book 22 June 1754–25 October 1760).

2 Biographies

Felice Giardini: early years in England

The known facts of Giardini's career before he settled in England can be briefly summarized. Born in Turin on 12 April 1716 of French parentage, he was sent as a chorister to Milan Cathedral where he studied singing, composition and harpsichord with Giuseppe Pietro Paladini, whose students also included Giovanni Battista Sammartini.[1] However, 'having previously manifested a disposition and partiality for the violin, his father recalled him to Turin, in order to receive instructions on that instrument of the famous *Somis*'.[2] According to Pohl, Giardini moved to Rome at the age of twelve; two years later he obtained a place among the *ripieni* in the orchestra of the Teatro San Carlo in Naples and soon rose through the ranks to become deputy leader. In about 1748 he set out on a concert tour of Germany where, on a visit to Berlin, he made music with Frederick the Great of Prussia, whom he regarded as a much better flautist than J. J. Quantz, the king's tutor on the instrument.[3] Giardini then travelled to England by way of France.

---

1 C. F. Pohl, *Mozart und Haydn in London*. 2 vols. (Vienna: Carl Gerold's Sohn, 1867), 1:170; Bertil H. van Boer, *Historical dictionary of music of the classical period* (Plymouth: Scarecrow Press, 2012), 425.
2 Charles Burney, *A general history of music from the earliest ages to the present period*. 4 vols. (London: for the author, 1776–89), 4:521; this was undoubtedly Giovanni Battista Somis and not his brother Giovanni Lorenzo, as both Burney (*General history*, 3:562) and Pohl (*Mozart*, 1:171) state. According to Burney, G. B. Sammartini was 'one of Giardini's masters on the violin'; see Abraham Rees, *The cyclopaedia, or, universal dictionary of arts, sciences, and literature*. 39 vols. (London: Longman, Hurst, Rees, Orme & Brown, 1819–20), 22: [no pagination] *s.v.* Martini, Giovanni Batista [*sic*] San.
3 Burney, *General history*, 4:522; [Anon.], 'Memoir of Felice Giardini', *The Harmonicon* 5 (1827), 215–17; Simon McVeigh, *The violinist in London's concert life 1750–1784: Felice Giardini and his contemporaries* (New York and London: Garland Publishing, 1989), 149, footnote 11.

10 *Biographies*

In 1750 he was in Paris, playing his own compositions at the Concert Spirituel – concertos on 24 and 28 March, and duets on 26 March and 3 April with the violinist (and later music publisher) Jean Baptiste Venier.[4] The date of Giardini's arrival in England has long been a matter of dispute. There is nothing to support the claims made by Fétis that the composer came to London in 1744, went to Paris in 1748 and returned to London eighteen months later.[5] Less easily dismissed are Burney's various pronouncements on the subject, for he claimed to have been present at Giardini's début; however, the dates he gives for that event (1749 and 1750) are not only mutually exclusive, but are irreconcilable with other evidence of a more trustworthy nature.[6] Corroborating Burney to some degree, although just as problematic, is the theory advanced by Roger Fiske, according to whom 'Giardini had been invited to England some years earlier by Frederick, Prince of Wales; he probably replaced the Prince's music director, Giuseppe Sammartini, who died in 1750'.[7] Fiske omitted to reference the source of this information, and no evidence to support his assertion has yet come to light; certainly there is no mention of Giardini in the Duchy of Cornwall's accounts for the period 1745–51, held on microfilm at the British Library, or among the Georgian papers at the Royal Library, Windsor Castle.[8]

The earliest references to Giardini in the London press appear on 26 April 1751, when the *General Advertiser* announced that 'A Benefit of Signor GUADAGNI, For the Profit of Signora CUZZONI' would take place next day at the New or 'Little' Theatre in the Haymarket. According to the programme printed in the newspapers, each half of the concert began with an 'Overture of Signor de Giardino', and he played two of his own concertos as well as a

---

4 Constant Pierre, *Histoire du Concert Spirituel 1725–1790* (Paris: Société française de Musicologie, 2000), 257–58.
5 François-Joseph Fétis, *Biographie universelle des musiciens et bibliographie générale de la musique*. 8 vols. (2nd edn, Bruxelles, 1860–65), 3:479–80.
6 cf. Burney, *General history*, 4:308, 460, 522 and 669; see below.
7 Roger Fiske, *English theatre music in the eighteenth century* (2nd edn, Oxford: Oxford University Press, 1986), 250.
8 Prince Frederick's Establishment Book 30 (Quarterly Accounts 1750–51) at Windsor mentions 'Mr Pardini a Musick Master', and it is possible his name was misread as 'Giardini'; I am grateful to Roberta Giubilini for this information. For the 'cellist Charles Pardini, see Philip H. Highfill Jr., Kalman A. Burnim and Edward A. Langhans, *A biographical dictionary of actors, actresses, musicians, dancers, managers & other stage personnel in London, 1660–1800*. 16 vols. (Carbondale and Edwardsville: Southern Illinois University Press, 1973–93), 11:196; and *Music and theatre in Handel's world: The family papers of James Harris 1732–1780*, ed. Donald Burrows and Rosemary Dunhill (Oxford: Oxford University Press, 2002), 19–20.

'Sonata del Signor St. Martini'. Burney attributed the thin house on the day to the aged Cuzzoni's failing voice, which was 'reduced to a mere thread':

> yet, when Giardini played a solo of Martini of Milan's composition, the applause was so long and loud, that I never remember to have heard such hearty and unequivocal marks of approbation at any other musical performance whatever.[9]

Burney describes the benefit as Giardini's 'first performance in public' and places it 'at the little theatre in the Hay-market' on 'May the 18th' 1750. In fact, there was no performance that day at the New Theatre, but there was one at the venue in Brewer Street, St James's, popularly known as Hickford's Room, where Cuzzoni gave the first of two concerts that month. Clearly Burney has conflated two Cuzzoni events a year apart, and it seems likely that his account of the audience's reaction to Giardini playing the Sammartini sonata relates to the concert at the New Theatre on 27 April 1751, when we know a work of that description was on the programme. All the evidence points to this as the date of Giardini's first public performance in this country.[10] Certainly, the wording used by the *Daily Advertiser* on the 26th instant to trailer that concert – 'We hear that Signior de Giardino[,] a celebrated Performer on the Violin, will perform at Mrs. Cuzzoni's Benefit Tomorrow Night, at the New Theatre' – suggests that he was a figure with whom London audiences had yet to become properly acquainted.[11]

Giardini made a living for himself in England not only as a player but also as a sought-after teacher of the violin and singing. According to Burney:

> Such was the state of Music in London ... when Giardini arrived, whose great hand, taste and style of playing, were so universally admired, that he had soon not only a great number of scholars on the violin, but taught many ladies of the first rank to sing; and after he had been here a few years, he formed a morning *academia*, or concert at his house,

---

9 Burney, *General history*, 4:308 and 460.
10 Burney's 1750 date persists to this day; see Stephanie Klauk and Rainer Kleinertz, 'Mozart's Italianate Response to Haydn's Opus 33', *Music & Letters* 97/4 (November 2016), 575–621, at 585.
11 Writing later of the same occasion, Burney adds that 'We had met [Giardini] the night before at a private concert, with Guadagni and Frasi, at the house of Napthali Franks, esq. who was himself one of the best dilettanti performers on the violin at that time'; see Rees, *The cyclopaedia*, 16: *s.v.* Giardini, Felice.

12 *Biographies*

composed chiefly of his scholars, vocal and instrumental, who bore a part in the performance.[12]

Giardini's violin pupils came from all walks of life, ranging from gentleman-amateurs – such as Sir William Hamilton, diplomat and art collector, whom he taught in the early 1750s – to aspiring professionals like Richard Hay/Hays, who had been one of Michael Festing's scholars until 1752.[13] It is easy to understand why he was in such demand as a teacher. Burney's description of Giardini's arrival on the London musical scene as 'a memorable æra in the instrumental Music of this kingdom' gives us some idea of the sensational impact his playing had on English audiences, 'who had never been accustomed to hear better performers than *Festing*, *Brown*, and *Collet*.'[14] In particular, Burney drew attention to 'His tone; bow; execution; graceful carriage of himself and his instrument', and later wrote:

> If ... surpassed by a few in taste, expression, and execution, his tone and graceful manner of playing are still unrivalled, nor does any one, of all the admirable and great performers on the violin, surpass all others so much at present, as Giardini did, when at his best, all the violinists in Europe.[15]

Burney hints at what was perhaps the most distinctive aspect of Giardini's playing – the beauty of his luminous and full-bodied tone; this quality was characteristic of the Piedmont school of violin-playing generally, and was emphasized time and again in the accounts of contemporaries who heard him perform. For instance, the composer, organist and writer on music Charles Avison, in his *Essay on Musical Expression* (1753), gives a somewhat lukewarm appraisal of the playing of two of Giardini's early contemporaries and continues:

> But if we would hear these Qualities united in their full Perfection, we must repair to the admired GIARDINI. The Brilliancy and Fullness of his Tone, the Sweetness, Spirit, and Variety of his Expression, his amazing Rapidity of Execution, and Exuberance of Fancy, joined with the most

---

12 Burney, *General history*, 4:669–70.
13 See *Daily Advertiser* 25 March 1754 for details of a concert at the Great Room in Dean Street, Soho, 'For the Benefit of Signor and Signora Degiardino'; this included 'A Solo on the Violin by Master Hays, Pupil to the late Mr. Festing, and, since his Death, a Pupil of Sig. Degiardino's'.
14 *General history*, 4:460 and 522.
15 Burney, in Rees, *The cyclopaedia*, 16: s.v. 'Giardini, Felice'.

perfect Ease and Gracefulness in the Performance, concur to set him at the Head of his Profession.[16]

According to W. T. Parke, 'Giardini, when in his zenith, produced on the violin a tone more powerful and clear than any of his contemporaries';[17] and the composer and viola player William Shield said that he 'had the finest tone he ever heard, when the strength of it was considered'.[18] The author of an anonymous pamphlet drew attention to his 'mellifluous tone, knowledge of bowing, and of the finger-board of the violin', and wrote of his pupil Hay that he was 'a tolerable imitator of Giardini's tone and manner'.[19]

Giardini may also have supplemented his income by dealing in violins. His ability to elicit a beautiful sound from indifferent instruments was one he learned to exploit financially, according to Parke:

> This knack ... proved very profitable to Giardini, enabling him to sell his inferior instruments at a large price to gentlemen, who, in his hands, admired their powerful tone; though they found afterwards, to their great surprise, that they could draw forth very little, apparently not aware that the tone came from the skill used, not from the fiddle.[20]

Thomas Gainsborough, the most musically inclined of English painters and a close friend of Giardini's, tells a similar story in a letter to James Unwin in 1765:

> you put me in mind of a little Fiddle that Giardini pick'd up here in Bath, which nobody would think well of, because there was nobody who knew how to bring out the tone of, and which ... in his Hands produced the finest Music in the World.[21]

---

16 The violinists in question were Knerler and Carbonelli; see *Charles Avison's* Essay on Musical Expression *with related writings by William Hayes and Charles Avison*, ed. Pierre Dubois (Aldershot: Ashgate, 2004), 44–45.
17 William Thomas Parke, *Musical memoirs*. 2 vols. (London, 1830), 1:154–55.
18 Joseph Farington, *The Farington diary*, ed. J. Greig. 8 vols. (London: Hutchinson, 1922–28), 1:238.
19 *A B C Dario Musico* (Bath, 1780), 22 and 26.
20 *Musical memoirs*, 1:155.
21 *The letters of Thomas Gainsborough*, ed. John Hayes (New Haven, CT, and London: Yale University Press for the Paul Mellon Centre for Studies in British Art, 2001), 37 (20). The way the composer, organist and amateur painter William Jackson of Exeter recalled what was probably the same incident depicts Gainsborough in a somewhat naïve light. Having heard Giardini play a particular violin at Bath, the painter 'was frantic until he possessed the *very* instrument which had given him so much pleasure – but seemed much surprized

London's cultural life during the eighteenth and most of the nineteenth centuries was largely determined by 'the season', that is, that time of year during which the aristocracy and gentry came to town for political, economic or social reasons, and/or to indulge in the city's commercialized leisure facilities. This period ran from November to May and coincided roughly with the royal family's residence at court, parliamentary sessions and the sitting of the law courts. However, by early summer the metropolitan élite had decamped to their country estates or some provincial resort in search of rural refreshment or a change of scene. To earn a living during this dead season, when the concert halls and theatres were dark, many of the capital's foreign musicians toured the provinces, visiting fashionable spa towns such as Bath and Scarborough or regional centres like Bristol and York. In the latter city, concerts were held during the summer Assize week and the August Race week, and it did not take long for a player of Giardini's stature to find gainful employment out of season. On 20 August 1751 he took part in a concert of vocal and instrumental music 'For the BENEFIT of the MUSICK-ASSEMBLY, at the Rooms in Blake-Street, York'; the other performers included James Nares, organist of the Minster, and two London-based musicians – mezzo-soprano Caterina Galli and the 'cellist Mr Beneke.[22] Two days later Giardini had a benefit concert at the same venue; thus began an association with the north-east of England that he would renew almost annually for the next twenty-five or so years.[23]

It may have been at one of these Race week concerts that Giardini was introduced to a patron who would turn out to be his principal benefactor, namely the redoubtable Harriet Fox Lane (1705–71). She inherited a reputed £100,000 and extensive landed property as the only legitimate heir of Robert Benson, Member of Parliament for York and later first Baron Bingley (d. 1731). He had been a founding Director, and later Deputy Governor, of the Royal Academy of Music, a joint-stock company set up in 1719 to secure the financial future of Italian opera in London with Handel as 'Master of the Orchestra'. When the company disbanded in 1728, Bingley took the lead in establishing the so-called 'Second Academy' (1729–34)

---

that the music of it remained behind with Giardini!'; see *The four ages; together with essays on various subjects* (London, 1798), 148.

22 David Garrick refers to a performance by 'ye famous Geortini' in York on 20 August; see *The letters of David Garrick*, ed. David M. Little and George M. Kahrl. 3 vols. (London: Oxford University Press, 1963), 1:175. Giardini and Galli took part in Beneke's benefit at Hickford's Room on 17 February 1752.

23 *York Courant* 20 August 1751; Rosemary Southey, 'Commercial music-making in eighteenth-century north-east England: A pale reflection of London?' 2 vols. (Ph.D. dissertation, University of Newcastle, 2001), 1:70.

with Handel and Johann Jakob Heidegger; he also maintained three musicians as part of his household, and hosted musical evenings at his London residence in Cavendish Square.[24] Bingley's estate included what is perhaps his most enduring monument, Bramham Park – a grand and unusual house between Leeds and Wetherby in West Yorkshire that was the subject of a lengthy pastoral poem by Francis Fawkes in 1745.[25] A few months after her father's death Harriet married George Fox, who in 1751 added 'Lane' to his surname on inheriting the Irish estates of his uncle, Viscount Lanesborough. MP for York from 1742 to 1761 and Lord Mayor in 1757, Lane was created Baron Bingley in 1762, when his father-in-law's extinct title was revived for him. Burney mentions Harriet as one of the patrons who organized private concerts in the early 1750s:

> The next remarkable *Academia* ... was established at the house of Mrs. Fox Lane, afterwards Lady Bingley, on the arrival of Giardini in England. The superior talents of that performer were always warmly patronised by this lady to the time of her death; and not content with admiring him herself, she contrived every means that could be devised to make him the admiration of others. As Giardini was seldom to be heard in public after his first arrival, she invited very select parties of the first people in the kingdom to hear him at her house, for which happiness she did not suffer them to remain ungrateful at his benefit.[26]

Harriet's love of music, and particularly her admiration for Italian castrati, has led to her being identified with the subject of a sonnet entitled 'On a Raptur'd Lady', who apparently exclaimed from her box in the theatre:

---

24 See Judith Milhous and Robert D. Hume, 'New light on Handel and the Royal Academy of Music in 1720', *Theatre Journal* xxxv/2 (1983), 149–67; *Handel's trumpeter: The diary of John Grano*, ed. J. Ginger (New York: Pendragon Press, 1998), 14 and 211; Elizabeth Gibson, 'The Royal Academy of Music (1719–1728) and its Directors', in *Handel tercentenary collection*, ed. Stanley Sadie and Anthony Hicks (London: Macmillan, 1987), 138–64; *Oxford dictionary of national biography* (henceforth *ODNB*), s.v. Benson, Robert, Baron Bingley (bap. 1676, d. 1731); *George Frideric Handel: Collected documents*, ed. Donald Burrows, Helen Coffey, John Greenacombe and Anthony Hicks. 5 vols. (Cambridge: Cambridge University Press, 2013–), 1 (1609–1725):425 *et seq.*, and 2 (1725–34):268 *et seq.*

25 The poem was dedicated to Robert Lane (1732–68), Harriet's only son.

26 Burney, *General history*, 4:671. The lady satirised in *The Connoisseur*, 4/128 (1757), 183–89 for her concerts and 'unquenchable rage after musical compositions' was almost certainly Lady Bingley.

16 *Biographies*

'One God! One Farinelli!'²⁷ An eighteenth-century tradition also connects her with the lady in William Hogarth's 'La Toilette', the fourth plate in his *Marriage à la mode* series (1745), who is depicted in an ecstatic state as she listens to the singing of a castrato now thought to be Senesino.²⁸ Harriet's enthusiasm for Italian music and musicians was at times to the detriment of native performers and other art forms, as the actor and theatre manager John Jackson (1729/30–1806) ruefully recalled:

> I addressed a very polite card to each of these noble personages, requesting their patronage, and signifying that I would do myself the honour of waiting on them personally for their answers. I was informed by Lady Bingley's gentlewoman, that "her Ladyship could not be seen. It will be needless for you, Sir, to call again. I read your card, and am ordered by my Lady to acquaint you, that her Ladyship never encourages any actors [*sic*] benefit." She could lavish hundreds, however, upon those of Italian singers.²⁹

Harriet inherited from her father not only a passion for music but also a talent for landscape design, and she and her husband were responsible for building most of the temples in the grounds at Bramham Park. The Lanes were also keen followers of the turf, and there are press reports of them attending the 1751 York and Doncaster meetings, 'amongst many other Persons of Distinction'.³⁰ Tate Wilkinson, actor and manager of the Theatre Royal, York, remembered his encounter with Harriet during the 1765 Race week, when Giardini was in town:

> About twelve on the Wednesday, when I had finished the rehearsal of the Provoked Wife, a deputation of gentlemen were sent as ambassadors

---

27 See Austin Dobson, *William Hogarth* (London: Sampson Low, Marston and Co. Ltd., 1893), 100; and Gladys Wilson, "One God! One Farinelli!' Amigoni's portraits of a famous *castrato*', *Apollo* 140 (September 1994), 45–51. 'On a Raptur'd Lady' was printed in the *Daily Journal* on 6 June 1735. According to Horace Walpole, the lady in question was Lady Rich; see Ronald Paulson, *Hogarth's graphic works* (3rd rev. edn, London: The Print Room, 1989), 93.
28 See *British biography: Or, an accurate and impartial account of the lives and writings of eminent persons in Great Britain and Ireland*. 10 vols. (London, 1777), 10:354; and John Nichols, *Biographical anecdotes of William Hogarth* (London, 1781), 106; Paulson, *Hogarth's graphic works*, 120.
29 John Jackson, *The history of the Scottish stage from its first establishment to the present time* (Edinburgh, 1793), 49–50. Mrs Fox Lane, however, did subscribe to the publication of Lord Henry Hyde's comedy *The Mistakes; or, the Happy Resentment* (London, 1758).
30 *General Advertiser* 31 August, and *Whitehall Evening Post or London Intelligencer* 28 September–1 October.

from the ladies assembled then at Giordani's [*recte* Giardini's] concert. York races were then in their high glory. Giordani was at that time under the patronage of Lady Bingley, who had great sway in that town and county, and was really enthusiastically musical; she settled £200 a year on him; which annuity he enjoys to this day, and will to the end of his life.[31]

The gentlemen had been sent to inform Wilkinson that, while Harriet and the other ladies were minded to patronize his establishment that evening, they would not come to 'so indecent a play as the Provoked Wife', and would attend only if he replaced it with 'another comedy'. He acquiesced to this 'command from the boxes' and put on Arne's comic pasticcio *Love in a village* instead. This was not the first occasion on which Lady Bingley asserted her position as self-appointed guardian of public morality, as we shall discover.

Giardini's summer tours of northern England during the 1750s were often made in the company of female singers. In 1752 he shared the concert platform with Galli and the soprano Giulia Frasi at a benefit for the York Music Assembly on 13 August, and took a benefit for himself the next day.[32] In July of the following year he was in county Durham with the soprano Violante Vestris (*c*.1725–91), having been escorted by Mrs Lane from Bramham to Gibside, near Gateshead, where they stayed as guests of the Bowes, one of the richest and most influential landed families in the north-east. George Bowes, coal baron and Member of Parliament for the county, was a patron of Giardini's friend Charles Avison, who was based in Newcastle upon Tyne.[33] The musicians gave a private concert in Gibside's Banqueting House on 21 July, and later performed in the Assembly Room in Durham at Race week concerts managed by the local organist and composer John Garth.[34] The couple then made their way south to York, where Vestris

---

31 Tate Wilkinson, *Memoirs of his own life*. 4 vols. (York, 1790), 4:17. It is clear from the *Public Advertiser* for 23 September 1784 that it was Giardini who received the £200 annuity. Wilkinson similarly confuses 'Giordani' with 'Guadagni' in discussing the cast of John Christopher Smith's *The Fairies* (1755); *Memoirs*, 4:202. Thomas Wilkes, too, refers to 'the Giardino family' when he means 'the Giordani family'; see *A general view of the stage* (London, 1759), 52.
32 *York Courant* 11 August 1752.
33 *Charles Avison in context: National and international musical links in eighteenth-century north-east England*, ed. Roz Southey and Eric Cross (Abingdon: Routledge, 2018), 8. Bowes's wife Mary subscribed to James Nares, *Eight setts of lessons for the harpsichord* (1747); see Margaret Seares, 'The composer and the subscriber: a case study from the 18th century', *Early Music* 39/1 (February 2011), 65–78, at 75.
34 See *Newcastle Courant* 21 July 1753, advertising concerts on 26th and 27th of the month. The visit to Gibside is mentioned in Emily J. Climenson, *Elizabeth Montagu, Queen of the*

18 *Biographies*

had a benefit at Blake Street on 22 August; Giardini led the ensemble, with support from James Nares (harpsichord), Messrs Hey and Onofrio (second violin), and Garth (violoncello). 'Mr. Hey' was possibly Richard Hay; as one of Giardini's pupils at the time, he may have accompanied him on tour, playing when required and carrying out menial tasks as any apprentice might do for his master.[35] No details of the programme survive, but it is possible that Giardini performed one of his *Sei sonate di cembalo con violino o flauto traverso* Opus 3 at this concert, for the first page of a British Library copy of the score is signed and dated 'J. Nares 1753'.[36]

Giardini and Vestris were evidently staying with the Lanes at Bramham Park at this stage in their itinerary, for it was there in the local parish church that the couple were wed. On 28 August 1753 'Felice Giardini Gent: of Bramham Park in the Diocese of York aged above 24 Years', and Violante Vestris, 'of the same place ... aged above 22 Years and a spinster', were married by licence, the groom having earlier in the day signed a printed allegation and bond in standard form swearing that there was no impediment to the union, and promising to pay the sum of £200 if the licence was not complied with (see Illustrations 2.1 and 2.2).[37] The correspondence of Spencer Cowper, dean of Durham at the time, throws additional light on the circumstances under which the knot was tied. After noting with some amusement that the *London Evening Post* had twice reported the marriage of his niece Lady Caroline Cowper on different dates several weeks apart, the dean writes:

> This Second Match of L'y Car's [Lady Caroline's] puts me in mind of Giardini and Vestris. Mr. Bowes at Gibside found this lovely Couple in Bed together, which did not a little raise his Choler. They pleaded

---

Blue-Stockings: Her correspondence from 1720 to 1761. 2 vols. (London: Murray,1906), 2:37, where Giardini's name is wrongly transcribed 'Jordain'; the original letter, now in the Huntington Library, San Marino, California (call-mark MO 2284), has 'Jordani'. Giardini, Avison, Mrs Lane and Mrs Bowes were among the subscribers to Garth's eight-volume collection of *The first fifty psalms set to music by Benedetto Marcello* (London: John Johnson, 1757).

35 *York Courant* 21 August 1753. The roles of student and servant often coalesced. Document 4 mentions another Giardini pupil, the composer and violinist '(7) ... Gio: Batt: Noferi[,] the Complainant's then Servant', who gave Cox a receipt for £21 on his teacher's behalf in June 1753. This pre-dates by four years the earliest reference hitherto discovered to Noferi in England; see *New Grove Dictionary of music and musicians* (henceforth *NGD*). 29 vols. (2nd edn, London: Macmillan, 2001), 18:15–16, *s.v.* 'Noferi, Giovanni Battista'.
36 Call-mark: Hirsch III. 225.
37 Borthwick Institute for Archives, York: PR/BRAM 1 (Bramham parish registers 1586–1786); Borthwick Institute, York Diocesan Archive: MB G 1753 (Marriage Bond: Felice Giardini and Violante Vestris, 1753). The Thomas Swaine who signed the bond with Giardini was vicar of Bramham.

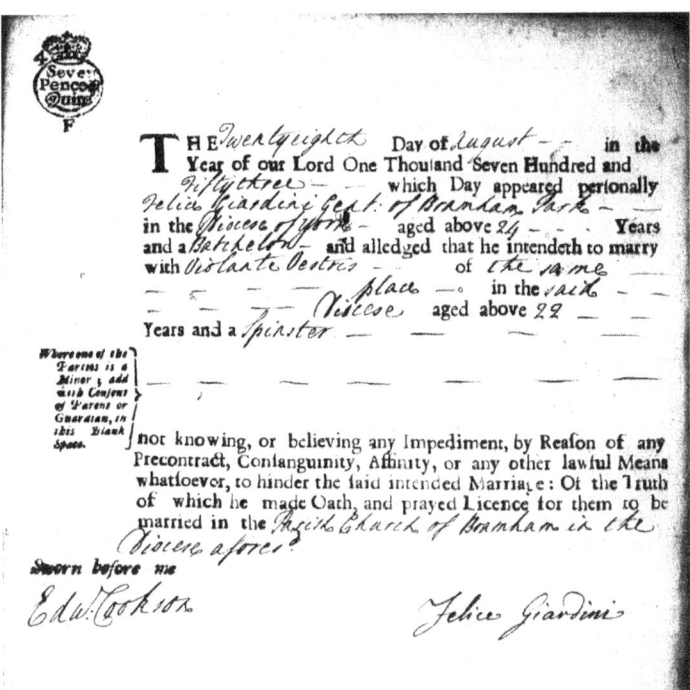

Illustration 2.1 Felice Giardini and Violante Vestris – marriage allegation. Reproduced with the permission of the Borthwick Institute for Archives, University of York.

Marriage. But this plea so little satisfy'd the penetrating Mrs Lane, tho' it did Bowes, that when they return'd with her to Bramum she made them be married over agin [sic]; and the Nuptials were repeated there with great Pomp and feasting.[38]

The newly-weds did not return to London immediately but remained in the area for some weeks, doubtless taking part in local musical activities, both private and public. Numerous shire towns and provincial cities in England had their own winter season of assemblies, plays, music meetings and oratorios. At York, regarded by many as the cultural capital of northern gentility, the attractions were specifically designed to rival those of London, Bath and Tunbridge Wells. Many of the nobility and gentry spent the winter

---

38 Letter dated 30 September 1753; see *Letters of Spencer Cowper, dean of Durham, 1746–74*, ed. Edward Hughes. Publications of the Surtees Society 165 (1956 for 1950), 168.

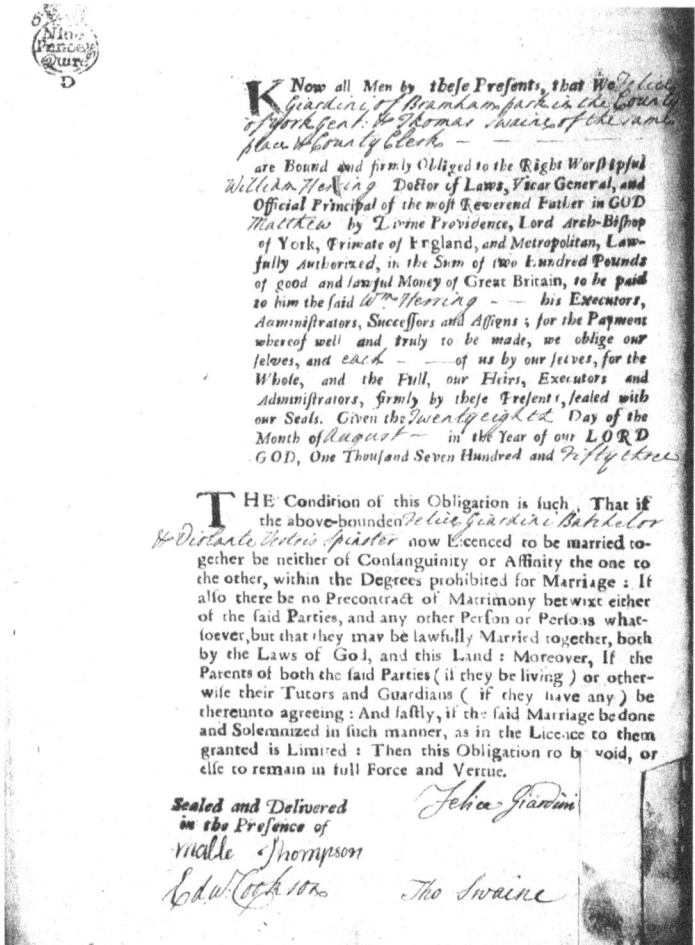

Illustration 2.2 Felice Giardini and Violante Vestris – marriage bond. Reproduced with the permission of the Borthwick Institute for Archives, University of York.

season there, and the provision of both dramatic representations and music was timed to coincide with their residency. Beginning in October, the series of concerts promoted by the Musick Assembly were given weekly on Friday evenings, ten before Christmas and ten afterwards, the season usually finishing by the middle of April. At the instigation of Mrs Lane, no doubt, 'Signor … and Signora Giardini' gave the second of the winter series

of subscription concerts at the Great Rooms in Blake Street on Friday 19 October.[39]

Giardini's marriage to Vestris was apparently of brief duration, and their last engagement together was on 4 April 1754 at a benefit organized for Mrs Ogle, the manager of the concert venue in Dean Street in London's Soho. They must have separated shortly thereafter, for Violante is recorded singing in Paris a year later under the name of 'Mme. Vestris de Giardini'.[40] As for Felice, he was back in York with Frasi between 20 and 23 August 1754, when they each took a benefit and gave two joint concerts.[41] That same year, according to Burney, 'he was placed at the head of the opera band; in which he introduced a new discipline, and a new style of playing, much superior in itself, and more congenial with the poetry and music of Italy, than the languid manner of his predecessor Festing'.[42] *A B C Dario* sheds light on what Burney might have meant by the 'new discipline':

> It would have been inexcusable to have forgotten [Giardini's] ability as a leader. He is the only person who, to attain the *same kind of expression* in a passage, obliges *all* those who play from *one part* to *bow alike*; and these strong proofs of his feelings and judgment, he extends to the tenor and violoncello. His commands are so absolute, yet convincing, that it would be as criminal to neglect his motions, as for a Prussian soldier to step out of his rank.[43]

In 1755 Giardini's female companion on tour was the Italian mezzo-soprano Rosa Curioni who, since the previous autumn, had been engaged as *seconda donna* at the Italian Opera in London. Giardini did not come to York in the following summer, but sent in his place the castrato Giuseppe Ricciarelli, *primo uomo* at the King's Theatre, and the violinist Thomas Pinto, who was later to succeed him as leader there. Giardini's exact whereabouts at the time are not known, but it is likely that he was on the Continent recruiting singers for the Opera, having just taken over management of the King's Theatre with the Austro-Italian singer Regina Mingotti. It has been suggested that he spent some time in north-east France, for – as Simon

---

39 *York Courant* 16 October 1753.
40 Pierre, *Histoire du Concert Spirituel*, 269. She retained the name when she sang the role of Egeria in Jommelli's pastorale *Il Trionfo d'Amore* at the Herzogliches Schloss, Ludwigsburg, in 1763; see the word-book in *US-Wc*.
41 *York Courant* 20 August 1754.
42 Rees, *The cyclopaedia*, 16: *s.v.* 'Giardini, Felice'. Michael Christian Festing (1705–52) had led the King's Theatre orchestra since about 1737; see Burney, *General history*, 4:658–59.
43 *A B C Dario Musico*, 23.

McVeigh points out – the title-page of the Paris edition of his Opus 1 Solos describes him as 'Virtuoso di Camera' to the King of Poland. The monarch in question was Stanisław I who, after his deposition in 1736, lived in exile as the Duke of Lorraine and Bar at Lunéville, where he presided over a court that became famous as a cultural centre until his death thirty years later.[44] There can be little doubt that Giardini's continental travels also took him to Paris – almost certainly with a view to replacing his London publisher John Cox, with whom he had recently fallen out.

John Cox: music trader and publisher

The biographies of John Cox, his wife and her first husband – the musical instrument-maker, publisher and engraver John Simpson – are so intertwined from a personal and business perspective that they need to be dealt with together. Simpson may be identified with the child baptized at St Bartholomew the Great, West Smithfield, on 4 June 1710, the son of Manuell and Dorathy.[45] He appears to have been apprenticed to the Hares, a long-established family of London music printers and publishers, who also made and sold musical instruments in Birchin Lane, off Cornhill. A year after Joseph Hare's death in 1733 Simpson, having reached the minimum age for freedom of the City, established his own business at the sign of the Viol and Flute in Sweeting's (or Swithin's) Alley, a narrow thoroughfare running along the east side of the Royal Exchange.[46] The importance of the Royal Exchange as the financial and commercial heart of the British empire during the eighteenth century and beyond has never been in doubt. Rather less well known is that this same area was also once one of the major centres of the London book trade, comparable in importance to St Paul's Churchyard and Pater Noster Row in pre-Restoration times.[47] The book trade here was extensive and varied, and a number of distinct strands of publishing supported a dense population of bookstores. A shop in this location, with its cosmopolitan ethos and access to traders with contacts in international markets, would have been considered a prime site from which to do business.

---

44 McVeigh, *The violinist*, 149. Giardini is not mentioned in Albert Jacquot, *La musique en Lorraine: Étude rétrospective d'après les archives locales* (2nd edn, Paris: A. Quantin, 1882).
45 London Metropolitan Archives (henceforth LMA): P69/BAT3/A/002/MS06778, Item 001 (St Bartholomew the Great, Register of Baptisms 1681–1715/6).
46 *Country Journal or the Craftsman* for Saturday 9 November 1734.
47 Laurence Worms, 'The Book Trade at the Royal Exchange', in *The Royal Exchange*, ed. Ann Saunders (London: London Topographical Society Publication 152, 1997), 209–26.

On 2 April 1736 'John Simpson of S*ain*ᵗ Bartho*lomew*ˢ the Great' married Ann Briscoe, spinster, in that area outside the Fleet prison known as the 'Rules' or 'Liberties'.[48] Ann was aged eighteen at the time, having been baptized at St Leonard's Shoreditch on 8 January 1718, the daughter of Henry and Ann.[49] The ceremony was 'irregular' in that it took place away from the home parishes of the spouses, and was performed without a licence, the calling of banns or parental consent, but their union was not considered invalid. Having in effect presented his in-laws with a *fait accompli*, Simpson nonetheless entered into a marriage bond and allegation with Ann's father on 1 June following, and two days later the couple were married in accordance with the rites of the established church at St Michael Queenhithe.[50] The church register gives Simpson's parish as 'Sᵗ Bartholomew Exchange London', and it was there that the newly-weds set up shop and spent the rest of their married life. They had a number of children, most of whom did not survive beyond infancy.[51]

Simpson died on 14 January 1749, away from home and apparently alone, in the parish of St Mary Stoke Newington. Because there were no witnesses to the will that he himself drafted, two friends had to appear and swear under oath that it was indeed in his hand before probate could be granted.[52] Simpson bequeathed everything to Ann, trusting that his 'Worldly Effects … will Maintain and support her and my dear Children in a good manner'. Two days after his funeral on 9 February the newspapers printed the following tribute, probably written by his widow:

> On Thursday Night was buried in a handsome Manner, at St. Bartholomew's Church behind the Royal-Exchange, Mr. John Simpson, who kept a Musical Instrument and Musick Shop in Swithin's-Alley, near the Royal-Exchange; a Man of strict Honour,

---

48 See The National Archives of Great Britain (henceforth TNA): RG7/144 and 147. RG7 preserves the registers of baptisms and clandestine marriages in the Fleet and King's Bench prisons, the May Fair Chapel and the Mint. It was not uncommon for such ceremonies to be entered more than once in these registers. The series records the nuptials of a significant proportion of the population of London and surrounding areas up to 1754; it has been estimated that in the first half of the eighteenth century a third of all marriages were actually clandestine.
49 LMA: P91/LEN/004/MS07496, Item 002 (St Leonard Shoreditch, Register of Baptisms July 1709–July 1727). The family may have been related to the bookseller and music publisher Samuel Briscoe (fl. 1690–1705).
50 See LMA: DL/A/24 MS10091E/49 and MS10091/76 (London and Surrey Marriage Bonds and Allegations 1597–1921); and LMA: P69/MIC6/A/008/MS09151, Item 001 (St Michael Queenhithe, Register of Marriages 1705–36).
51 Their sole surviving male heir John Pitt Simpson was baptized at St Bartholomew's on 21 July 1745; the registers make no mention of a son James, *pace NGD*, 23: 411, *s.v.* 'Simpson, John'.
52 See TNA: Prerogative Court of Canterbury (henceforth PCC Wills) PROB 11/768/125.

remarkable Industry, and universally beloved by all his Acquaintance: The Business, we can assure the Public, will be carried on by his Widow; so that all his former Customers, and others, that will favour her with their Custom, may be certain of having them executed in the best Manner.[53]

After a suitable period of mourning, Ann re-opened for business and produced her own 'Catalogue of new Musick Printed for and sold by the Widow of John Simpson'.[54] Fortunately, she did not have to run the shop entirely by herself, for she could draw on the support of Maurice Philips Whitaker, who later claimed to have been 'Assistant to the late Mr. SIMPSON, at his Music Shop in Sweeting's Alley, Cornhill, and chief Manager of that Business for several Years after his Death for the Widow; and Mr. COX, her second Husband'.[55]

John Cox has proved to be the most elusive of the main protagonists in this tale. It was Winton Dean who first suggested that the 'Mr. Cox' who sang for Handel on a number of occasions might also have been the music-seller and publisher.[56] This theory appears to derive support from an advertisement for a concert on 25 March 1757 in aid of the Lock Hospital, which included a performance by 'Mr. Cox, and others' of Johann Adolf Hasse's oratorio *I pellegrini*. Given Giardini's heavy involvement in that event – he not only supplemented Hasse's music with some of his own, but also led the orchestra and played a solo – it is tempting to identify the singer with his business associate.[57] However, for various reasons discussed below, their relationship would have been decidedly cool by then, making such speculation a remote possibility only. Donald Burrows similarly rejects this hypothesis, although on different grounds, suggesting more plausibly that 'Mr. Cox' was in fact Hugh Cox of the Chapel Royal.[58]

---

53 *London Gazetteer* Saturday 11 February 1749.
54 See British Library call-mark: 7896. h. 40. (21).
55 *Public Advertiser* 16 June 1764; see also Charles Humphries and William C. Smith, *Music publishing in the British Isles* (Oxford: Blackwell, 1970), 330.
56 Winton Dean, *Handel's dramatic oratorios and masques* (London: Oxford University Press, 1959), 188.
57 See *Public Advertiser* 16 and 25 March 1757; for a reproduction of the playbill listing the performers, see Janet K. Page, 'The hautboy in London's musical life, 1730–1770', *Early Music* 16/3 (August 1988), 359–71, at 364. For Giardini's long association with the Lock Hospital, see Simon McVeigh, 'Music and Lock Hospital in the 18th century', *The Musical Times* 129/1743 (May 1988), 235–40; and Nicholas Temperley, 'The Lock Hospital Chapel and its music', *Journal of the Royal Musical Association* 118/1 (1993), 44–72.
58 Donald Burrows, *Handel and the English Chapel Royal* (Oxford: Oxford University Press, 2005), 300.

Research into John Cox's biography has been hampered by the fact that his name was extremely common in mid-eighteenth-century London. Restricting oneself to the immediate vicinity of the Royal Exchange, one notes a John Cox (d. 1768) who was landlord of the Cock and Lion in St Michael's Alley, Cornhill; and even in Swithin's Alley itself there was a haberdasher/hatter/hosier of the same name, who was declared bankrupt in 1760, 1764 and 1768, and who later died in Madras. One might well question the relevance of such individuals to an investigation of the early biography of Cox the music publisher, but at a time of great fluidity and diversification in the labour market, when it was not unusual for people to construct portfolio careers in order simply to make ends meet, one dismisses the possibility of a multiple identity at one's peril. Indeed, one of the more likely candidates is the John Cox from Guildford, who in 1735 was apprenticed to Thomas Cox (d. 1754), a broker and bookseller at the Royal Exchange.[59]

Nothing for certain is known of John Cox until 10 November 1750 when he and widow Simpson married at St George's Chapel, Mayfair, another popular venue for clandestine weddings that catered not just for the working classes but also for professionals and the aristocracy.[60] For about six months after their marriage the couple continued to trade under the name of 'Simpson's', 'Ann/Mrs Simpson's', even 'Mr Simpson's', but from the spring of 1751 Cox's position within the business and his influence on its future direction become increasingly apparent from the newspapers. From the middle of March he mounted a sustained advertising campaign offering

---

59 See D. F. McKenzie, *Stationers' Company apprentices 1701–1800* (Oxford: The Oxford Bibliographical Society, N. S. 19, 1978), 92; and Ian Maxted, *The London book trades, 1735–1775: A checklist of members in trade directories and in Musgrave's 'Obituary'* (Exeter: J. Maxted, 1984), 9. The papers sometimes confuse Thomas Cox with John; see the advertisements for Giardini's *Sei sonate* and Besozzi's *Six sonatas* in the *London Daily Advertiser* for 16 December 1751 and 3 April 1752, respectively. Thomas's will is in TNA: PCC Wills; PROB 11/806/338; he is remembered today for publishing an abridgement of *Robinson Crusoe* (1719) in close chronological proximity to the original, thereby igniting a well-documented war of words between himself and Defoe's publisher William Taylor, who considered the act of abridgement to be illegal and immoral. There was also a Thomas Samuel Cox, stationer, at 6 Sweeting's Alley, Cornhill, in 1779–1782; see Maxted, *The London book trades*, 55.
60 See TNA: RG7/248, and *The register of baptisms and marriages at St. George's Chapel May Fair*, ed. George J. Armytage (London: Harleian Society Publications 15, 1889), 177; Humphries and Smith, *Music publishing*, 120; Dean, *Handel's dramatic oratorios*, 188; Highfill et al., *Biographical dictionary*, 4:19; and *NGD*, 23: 411, *s.v.* 'Simpson, John' erroneously give the year as 1751. Lord Hardwicke's Marriage Act, which came into effect in 1754, put an end to such 'common law' marriages, although couples could still travel to other areas of the United Kingdom not covered by the act.

for sale 'all the newest MUSICK', including publications from the Simpson back-catalogue. When he produced his own 'Catalogue of new Musick' (*c*.1752), the listed items were to be 'Printed for and sold by JOHN COX at Simpson's Musick Shop at the Bass Viol & Flute in Sweetings Alley opposite the East Door of the Royal Exchange LONDON'.[61] Early in 1753 he brought out a much fuller version of the same list, a copy of which is preserved at the back of British Library call-mark: Hirsch III.225 – Giardini's *Sei sonate* Opus 3.[62] Apart from printed music, Cox dealt in new and second-hand instruments, offering 'READY MONEY for Old HARPSICHORDS and SPINNETS' as well as 'a great Choice of all Sorts of Musical Instruments, by the best Masters'.[63] He also sold strings, as John Simpson had done in the 1740s when he was a major importer of 'right Roman ring Strings for Violins, Violoncellos, and Double Basses'.[64] It is easy to see why a foreign musician like Giardini, newly arrived in London, would repair to Cox's well-stocked emporium to supply his professional needs.

Newspaper advertisements suggest that Cox transacted business from the same premises that the Simpsons had occupied since the 1730s, the address of which is confirmed as 'Sweetings Alley Cornhill' by the Sun insurance policy he took out in March 1751. There 'his hous*ehol*^{d} Goods Utensils *and* Stock in Trade in his now dwell*in*^{g} house only Brick situate as aforesaid' were valued at £700.[65] However, conditions in the shop must have been cramped, for as early as 1742 Simpson had found it necessary to rent additional floor space from tradespeople in the Royal Exchange who sublet their spare capacity. Cox abandoned this arrangement on taking over, renting instead directly from the Exchange. He insured 'his Utensils *and* Stock in his Shop and Warehouse over only under the Royal Exchange in the said Alley' for £500, and paid an annual rent of £18 for this new space. Here he was a close neighbour of the distinguished watchmaker and scientist John Ellicott and his son Edward, one of whom is mentioned in Schedule A1.[66] For a while the Coxes appear to have maintained a second shop in London,

---

61 The British Library copy – call-mark: 7896.h.40 (3) – is misdated *c*.1755.
62 Occasional reference is made to this catalogue and its prices when discussing the musical items listed in Schedule A1 (Appendix 1); see Chapter 5, *s.v.* 'Music purchases'.
63 *London Daily Advertiser and Literary Gazette* 19 March 1751; *General Advertiser* 7 June 1751.
64 *London Evening Post* 22–24 April 1746. Other music-sellers – including Elizabeth Hare, John Walsh, John Tyther, James Oswald and John Johnson – also sold strings, but not to the same extent.
65 See LMA: CLC/B/192/F/001/Ms11936/92, p. 67; and www.galpinsociety.org/galpinextras/GS_Whitehead&Nex_A_to_D.pdf.
66 LMA: CLA/062/01/45 (Gresham College and Royal Exchange Account Book 5: 1731–56); and *Gazetteer and New Daily Advertiser* 11 September 1764 (Gresham Committee

for an advertisement in the *Public Advertiser* for 7 June 1762 shows that 'Mr. John Cox, Musical-Instrument-Maker at the Harp and Crown opposite Bow-Church, Cheapside' served as a ticket outlet for Peter Pasqualino's forthcoming benefit at Ranelagh Gardens.[67]

Insurance records enable us to trace the Coxes' whereabouts over the next decade, for they contain information relating not only to their business premises but to their places of abode. Thus, we know that in October 1756 they moved to Stanmore in Middlesex, where they insured their house and personal effects for £400; and by January 1758 they had relocated to Kingsland, in the parish of St John at Hackney, which was then a healthy and agreeable suburb on the Old North Road out of London favoured by the nobility and the City's business community. Here they became fellow parishioners of the Ellicotts, and it was to this village, and their 'Dwelling house Only Brick Situate On Kingsland Green in Kingsland Road', that the couple eventually retired.[68]

Given the ruthlessly competitive nature of publishing in eighteenth-century London, it was almost inevitable that Cox would sooner or later succumb to some of the book trade's less edifying practices, in particular piracy. Indeed, his first publication – the *Easy and familiar airs* of May 1751 – was an unauthorized edition of Carlo Tessarini's *Il piacer delle dame*, a collection of twelve short pieces for violin or flute with basso continuo that had appeared in Paris a few years earlier. Cox subsequently pirated other French editions, including books of sonatas by Alessandro Besozzi, Giovanni Battista Patoni, Fabio Ursillo and Domenico Ferrari, even though their publishers claimed to have acquired copyright protection locally in the form of a 'Privilège du Roi'; so long as the original editions were produced abroad, the chances of Cox suffering any legal repercussions at home were remote. However, the unauthorized publication of pieces by a musician living and working in England at the time was a different matter. In 1752 the London-based flautist, trumpeter and composer Lewis Christian Austin Granom purchased a licence from the Crown to protect his compositional output from piracy.[69] On learning that the copyright he thought

---

advertisement for letting the shops at the Royal Exchange); see also *ODNB*, *s.v.* Ellicott, John (1702/3–72).
67 The 'Harp and Crown' was the address of the music seller, printer and publisher John Johnson who died in 1762, in which year his widow succeeded to the business.
68 See Lance Whitehead and Jenny Nex, 'The insurance of musical London and the Sun Fire Office 1710–1779', *Galpin Society Journal* 67 (March 2014), 181–274.
69 Helen Crown, 'Lewis Granom: His significance for the flute in the eighteenth century' (Ph.D. dissertation, Cardiff University, 2013), 38, believes that John Simpson had pirated

he had secured for his *XII New songs and ballads* Opus 4 (1752) had been breached, he placed the following indignant notice in the newspapers:

> Whereas Mr. Granom has been informed that a certain Master of a Musick Shop, bought one of Mr. Granom's Books of Songs, and carried the same immediately to an Engraver of Musick, with an Intent to pirate and vend the same, to the great Prejudice of the Author; therefore … Mr. Granom, in Consideration of those who may be concerned in the above Scandalous Undertaking, forwarns [*sic*] all such Persons to desist, for not only they who gave the Orders for this Unwarrantable Work to be done, but the Engravers, Printers, or Venders of the same, shall be prosecuted to the utmost Severity of the Law, Mr. Granom having his Majesty's Patent for all his Works in general.[70]

For various reasons this warning proved ineffectual, and Granom was left with no alternative but to sue out a bill of complaint in Chancery, petitioning the Court to grant him an injunction restraining the defendants 'from publishing or vending the said Books … or any part thereof'.[71] When the case came to court in May 1753 it emerged that the 'certain Master of a Musick Shop' was none other than John Cox, who had evidently reprinted four songs from Granom's collection and sold them to some of London's most prestigious music retailers, including Thomas Cahusac, Elizabeth Hare, Peter and Robert Thompson, Henry Waylett and James Oswald. However, Granom's case was not altogether watertight, and after three years of legal stalemate the Master of the Rolls threw it out of court.[72]

The Coxes remained in business until June 1764, when Ann's poor health forced them to sell up and retire. News of the impending closure of their shop quickly spread, and the papers reveal considerable jockeying for position among rival music sellers wishing to ingratiate themselves with the Simpson/Cox clientele. One of the first to make his pitch was Maurice Whitaker, their former assistant, who had allegedly traded on his own account since March 1760 and who, on the demise of Cox's business, begged

> Leave to acquaint the Public, and the Merchants in particular, that he carries on the same Business in every Branch thereof, at his Music

---

Granom's Opuses 1–3 in the 1740s, but there is no evidence to support this view. For more on royal licences, see Chapter 3.
70 *London Daily Advertiser* 8 December 1752.
71 TNA: C 12/2371/34.
72 For a full account of the litigation and the issues involved, see Cheryll Duncan, 'The law and the profits: Lewis Granom and the royal licence as a form of music copyright protection' (forthcoming).

Shop, the Sign of the Violin, under the North Piazza of the Royal Exchange; where he hopes to receive the Favour of their Commands, which will be most punctually and respectfully obeyed.[73]

Competing for the same custom was Henry Thorowgood who, on the same day as Whitaker's advertisement appeared, placed the following notice in the press:

To MERCHANTS, DEALERS, and Others

MR. COX, of Sweeting's-Alley, Royal-Exchange, Musical Instrument Maker, (with whom I served my Apprenticeship) having left off Trade, I humbly solicit the Favours of his Customers, who may depend on being supplied with all Sorts of Goods in the Musical Business, on the most reasonable Terms, at the Violin and Guittar, near Mercers-Chapel, Cheapside.[74]

The contents of the Sweeting's Alley shop and the remainder of its lease went under the hammer on 23 June.[75] The auctioneer's advertisement for the sale paints a vivid picture of the range of goods available from a music shop 'in full Trade' in mid-eighteenth-century London (see Illustration 2.3). The Coxes' impressive stock of instruments, printed music and engraved plates was dispersed among the city's most prominent retailers and publishers. Many items, including some by Giardini, were bought by Robert Bremner who, in an appendage to an advertisement for a collection of Vauxhall songs, lists the plates he had acquired from the sale (see Illustration 2.4). Thorowgood, too, snapped up 'a considerable Part of Mr. Cox's Musical Effects, at a late Public Sale', before moving from Cheapside into 'the late Mr. Curtis's Music-Shop in the North Piazza of the Royal-Exchange'. Other purchasers of the Simpson/Cox stock-in-trade included John Walsh, and Charles and Samuel Thompson.[76]

---

73 *Public Advertiser* 16 June 1764. However, it appears that Whitaker was merely the 'Servant or Shopman' of William Curtis, the real owner of the business; see *Public Advertiser* 17 August 1764, where Curtis publicly disowned him. Whitaker responded by announcing his intention of setting up shop 'near his former one'; see *Gazetteer and New Daily Advertiser* 20 August 1764.
74 *Gazetteer and New Daily Advertiser* 16 June 1764.
75 Cox's rent (£4 10s a quarter) was paid up to 10 October 1764; see LMA: CLA/062/01/46 (Gresham College and Royal Exchange Account Book, vol. 6: 1757–83).
76 *Gazetteer and New Daily Advertiser* 22 December 1764; Humphries and Smith, *Music publishing*, 120 and 363. An excellent account of the scramble to acquire Cox's business assets is included in David Lasocki, 'New light on eighteenth-century English woodwind

> To be SOLD by AUCTION,
> By Mr. BROWNING,
> At his Great Room in the Royal Exchange, on Tuesday the 26th Inftant, and the following Day,
>
> THE Remainder of the Leafe of the Dwelling-Houfe and Shop of that old and well-eftablifhed Mufick-Shop in Sweeting's-alley, Cornhill, (carried on many Years by Mr. Simpfon) now in the Occupation of Mrs. Cox, in full Trade, who will recommend all the Cuftomers to the Purchafer of the Leafe, her Health not permitting her to continue in Bufinefs. Alfo all the genuine Stock in Trade; confifting of feveral Thoufand curious engraved Copper and Pewter Plates, of the Works of the moft efteemed and eminent Mufick Mafters, together with a great Number of Mufick Books of the neweft and moft favourite Pieces, Songs, &c. Variety of curious Fiddles, Baffes, Violoncellos, Harpfichords, Dulcimers, Guitars, Mandolins, French Horns, and other Inftruments, particularly a remarkable fine Fiddle by Jacobus Stainer, 1671, efteemed worth 50 Guineas; an exceeding fine Cremona Tenor, 1673, a very valuable Steel Engine complete for filvering Strings of all Kinds, a large Parcel of very old fine feafon'd Air Wood for Fiddles, and other Inftruments, and various other Effects.
> The Whole may be viewed on Saturday the 23d, and to the Time of Sale, which will begin punctually at Twelve o'Clock. Catalogues to be had at the Place of Sale; at the Mufick-Shop aforefaid; and at Mr. Browning's, in Threadneedle-ftreet.

Illustration 2.3 Auction of John Cox's stock-in-trade. Courtesy of the British Library. *Lloyd's Evening Post* 20–22 June 1764.

Notwithstanding his moves to the then rural settings of Stanmore and Kingsland, Cox maintained links with the City and St Bartholomew Exchange, for both his daughters, Ann and Lucy, were baptized there on 22 June 1754 and 15 December 1756, respectively. Also, an entry in the St Bartholomew accounts for 29 June 1766 suggests that the churchwardens

---

makers from newspaper advertisements', *Galpin Society Journal* 63 (May 2010), 73–142, at 97–99.

> **NEW MUSIC.**
> *This Day is published, Price* 1 s.
>
> A Second Book of new SONGS by Miſs Wearman, Mr. Vernon, and Mr. Gilſon, at Vauxhall.
>
> Printed for R. Bremner, oppoſite to Somerſet Houſe in the Strand.
>
> Of whom may be had, lately publiſhed,
> The new Songs ſung this Seaſon at Ranelagh and Marybone.
>
> The Publiſher thinks it neceſſary to inform Dealers, and others, that he has purchaſed the Plates of the following Works, being a Part of the Stock in Trade of Simpſon's Muſic Shop, lately ſold by Auction.
>
> For Violins, &c.
> Giardini's Overtures,
> Martini of Milan's three
> French Horn Concertos,
> Corelli's 12 Trios, op 7.
> Martini of Milan's Trios,
> Gluck's Trios,
> Moſell's Duets,
> Noferi's eight Solos,
> Ferrari's Solos, op. 1.
> Teſſarini's Airs,
> Muſical Pocket Book.
>
> For German Flutes,
> Spourni's Trios,
> Granom's Duets,
> Tellemans Canon's,
> The delightful Pocket Companion, 12 Books.
> For the Harpſichord.
> Ruſh's ſix Leſſons,
> Sandoni's Leſſons.
> Handel's Water Muſic,
> Haſſe's favourite Concertos
> Geminiani's favourite Minuets.
>
> Giardini's Songs, Theſaurus Muſicus, for two, three, and four Voices, by Blow, Purcell, and others; Jackſon on the Harmony of Sounds.

Illustration 2.4 Robert Bremner's purchase of Cox's plates (part of an advertisement for *The New Songs sung by Miss Wearman ... at Vaux-Hall*). Courtesy of the British Library.

Public Advertiser 13 October 1764.

there called upon him to perform a sensitive task on their behalf, perhaps because of some personal or musical connection he had with the deceased and his family:

> By M^r: Cox for the Administratrix. 1 Year Sallary due to the late John Atfeild [*sic*] Organist at Lady day 1766   £20. 0. 0.[77]

---

77 LMA: MS 4383/3 (Churchwardens' accounts of St Bartholomew by the Exchange, 1744–74), fo. 192. Appointed organist of the parish in 1762, Atfield died in March 1766 and was succeeded by William Goodwin; see Donovan Dawe, *Organists of the City of London 1666–1850* (priv. pr.; 1983), 75 and 102.

Cox himself died in the summer of 1769. The death notices in *The Middlesex Journal or, Chronicle of Liberty* for 24–27 June include the following entry: 'After a lingering illness, at his house at Kingsland, Lieutenant and Adjutant John Cox, of the Middlesex militia.' That Cox had paramilitary connections comes as something of a revelation, but they are substantiated by the St Bartholomew registers, which record the burial of 'Cap*tain* John Cox' on 29 June 1769; the churchwardens' accounts for the same day also show the receipt of £2 3s 4d for the 'Ground and Bell for John Cox'.[78]

78 LMA: MS 4383/3, fo. 242v.

3 Early collaborations

On the face of it, Felice Giardini and John Cox were something of an odd couple. By the early 1750s the latter had taken over John Simpson's moderately successful music shop in the city of London and was looking to expand commercially as an instrument dealer, music seller and publisher. Giardini, on the other hand, was a recently arrived Italian composer and violin virtuoso in search of pastures new where he could consolidate the reputation he had established on the Continent. Yet they both quickly realized that their respective aims and objectives were in many ways complementary, and that any association that might develop between them could be mutually beneficial. It is no surprise, then, that within a matter of months of Giardini's arrival in England he and Cox had entered into a working arrangement that was to prosper for the next five years.

First publications

The earliest evidence of their joint enterprise appears on the title-pages of Giardini's Opuses 1 and 2. When Giardini arrived from France in the spring of 1751 he brought with him a number of works that had already been printed on the Continent, as well as many of the plates from which they had been produced. This imported repertoire included his *Sei sonate a violino solo e basso … Opera prima*, and the *Sei duetti a due violini … Opera seconda*. Once in London Giardini set about self-publishing these collections, selling them – according to their imprints – from 'his Lodgings at the golden Ball in Bow Street near Covent Garden and by [i.e. through] J. COX at SIMPSON's Musick Shop in Sweetings Alley'. Both prints have features that betray the continental origin of their plates: the French sign for the trill (+), for instance, is retained throughout; instructions regarding formal repeats are given in Italian; and the works themselves are dedicated to a

French count (Opus 1) and a Prussian prince (Opus 2).[1] The Exchequer litigation throws new light on the subsequent history of the plates. According to Document 1, Giardini '(7) ... put the (8) said John Cox in Possession of the engraved Plates and Copies thereof', although he mistakenly implies that these included the plates of his Opus 3 Sonatas as well, an error to which Cox, as the publisher of that work, was at pains to draw attention in his answer.[2] The 'engraved Plates and Copies thereof' that Giardini handed over therefore consisted of his Solos (Opus 1) and Duets (Opus 2) only, and the implication is that Cox was to use his contacts in the trade to arrange for their re-printing as and when required. An entry on Cox's second Schedule (A2) for an unspecified date in December 1751 records the proceeds from the sale at Simpson's shop of those copies of Opuses 1 and 2 that Giardini brought into the country, doubtless minus the retailer's cut:

By his own Solos and Duetts sold for him   £41 2s 0d[3]

Having exhausted this imported stock, Cox may have been asked to run off more copies, but before he could do so he had to redeem the plates from Customs, for which cost he debited Giardini's account on 23 December:

To Cash paid Customhouse Duty for his plates   £4 0s 0d[4]

Two further entries on Schedule A1 possibly relate to Giardini's Solos and Duets. On 28 January 1752, Cox charged him six guineas for '2 Ream of Imperial Paper' and five guineas for 'printing 200 Books blue Paper and Sticking'.[5] Since Cox's normal print run for a music book was one hundred copies, those sums may represent the re-printing costs of Opuses 1 and 2. Similarly,

---

1 Comte Lancelot Turpin de Crissé (1716–93) was a French general whose *Essai sur l'art de la guerre* (1754) was one of the most widely read studies of contemporary warfare; Prince Heinrich of Prussia (1726–1802) was a soldier and statesman and the homosexual younger brother of King Frederick II ('Frederick the Great').
2 For Cox's purchase of the rights to Opus 3, see below.
3 Both collections retailed at 10s 6d.
4 Schedule A1 under date 23 December 1751. Royal statutes to protect the English pewter trade, passed in the middle years of the sixteenth century, were still in place; see John Hatcher and T. C. Barker, *A History of British Pewter* (London: Longman, 1974), 77, 152 and 198. The importation of newly manufactured pewter goods was prohibited, but 'Pewter old' was allowed, although it was subject to customs duty; see Henry Crouch, *A complete view of the British customs* (London, 1745), 200 and 554.
5 Blue paper wrappers were used to cover books sold to the public; books were rarely offered at a price that included binding. The legal clerk who drafted the document probably mistook 'Stitching' for 'Sticking'.

Early collaborations 35

on 16 April 1753 he billed Giardini for £5 15s 6d for 'printing 100 Books of Solos and Paper Sticking', which can only refer to a later printing of Opus 1.

Having assisted in the production and distribution of Giardini's first two collections, Cox seized the opportunity of publishing his *Sei sonate di cembalo con violino o flauto traverso ... Opera terza* when it presented itself, despite his limited experience in the field. His decision to take this on was doubtless based on a shrewd appraisal of Opus 3 as a species of chamber music – sonatas for solo harpsichord with an accompaniment for the violin – that was new to English tastes, and therefore highly marketable. Initially Giardini may have tried to publish the work himself, as he had done Opuses 1 and 2, for there are grounds for identifying it with the 'Six Sonatas for a German Flute and Violin, with a Thorough Bass for the Harpsichord', for which he had regularly solicited subscriptions in the newspapers between 23 July and 9 October 1751 (see Illustration 3.1). Against such an identification one might argue that it is unclear from the title which set of sonatas the proposals allude to; after all, it mentions both a harpsichord with thorough bass, which is essential for Opus 1, and a German flute, which is optional in Opus 3. Yet there can be little doubt

> *This Day are Published,*
> PROPOSALS for Printing by SUBSCRIPTION,
> SIX SONATAS for a GERMAN FLUTE and VIOLIN, with a Thorough Bass for the Harpsichord.
> Composed by Sig. FESICE DEGIARDINO.
>
> CONDITIONS.
> 1. That the Price to Subscribers will be Half a Guinea, to be paid at the Time of Subscribing.
> 2. That the Book will be neatly engraved, and printed on good Paper.
> 3. That the Subscribers Names will be printed before the Work.
> 4. That the Book will be ready to be delivered by the Twelfth of October, 1751.
> Subscriptions are taken in at Simpson's Musick-Shop in Sweeting's-alley; at Mrs. Hare's, facing the Mansion-House; at Mr. Peter Thompson's, Musick-Seller in St. Paul's Church-yard; at Mr. Walsh's, in Catherine-street in the Strand; at Mr. Waylett's Shop in Exeter Change; by Mr. Crofs, at Oxford; and Mr. Wynn, at Cambridge.

Illustration 3.1 Subscription proposals for Giardini's *Sei sonate* Op. 3. Courtesy of the British Library.

London Daily Advertiser and Literary Gazette 23 July 1751.

that the notice relates to the latter collection: Giardini would hardly have called for subscriptions to publish a work that had already been engraved – and that rather obviously so – on the Continent; besides which, the second condition of the proposals makes it clear that the process of engraving had yet to be accomplished.[6] The advertisement's many ambiguities are perhaps attributable to the newspaper editor's lack of familiarity with the latest musical developments and his readiness to 'correct' an aberrant form of words. The composer's given name is wrongly spelled, of course, and the designated instrumental forces should, strictly speaking, read 'German Flute *or* Violin'; but more importantly, the advertisement subverts the priority given to the harpsichord in Giardini's title, which is indicative of a more equal relationship between the instruments, in favour of a traditional verbal formula that completely misrepresents the nature of the collection's novel compositional processes.[7]

For the general public a work entitled 'Six Sonatas for a German Flute and Violin, with a Thorough Bass for the Harpsichord' must have conjured up visions of an old-fashioned set of trio sonatas, an irony that would not have been lost on Giardini who prided himself on promoting the most modern Italian music of the day. Little wonder, then, that the proposals elicited a lukewarm response, and that the date on which the book was due for delivery to subscribers – 12 October – passed uneventfully. Disappointing as that may have been for the composer, it did not dampen Cox's enthusiasm for the project, which he subsequently supported by purchasing the rights to the collection. Giardini recalls the bare details of the sale near the beginning of his Exchequer bill:

> (6) ... and your Orator [i.e. the composer] further sheweth unto your Honors that your Orator in consideration of Thirty Pounds to him in Hand paid by John Cox of Sweetings Alley London Gentleman did

---

6 For more on publication by subscription, see Jenny Burchell, '"The first talents of Europe": British music printers and publishers and imported instrumental music in the eighteenth century', in *Concert life in eighteenth-century Britain*, ed. Susan Wollenberg and Simon McVeigh (Aldershot: Ashgate, 2004), 93–113; and William Weber, 'The musician as entrepreneur and opportunist, 1700–1914' in *The musician as entrepreneur 1700–1914: Managers, charlatans, and idealists*, ed. William Weber (Bloomington: Indiana University Press, 2004), at 10.

7 In some later advertisements for Opus 3 Cox retains 'German Flute *and* Violin', but he lists the harpsichord first to reflect its important new role; see *London Daily Advertiser* 16 April 1752. For an interesting perspective on the origins of the accompanied sonata, see Nicholas Baragwanath, 'Mozart's early chamber music with keyboard: Traditions of performance, composition and commodification' in *Mozart's chamber music with keyboard*, ed. Martin Harlow (Cambridge: Cambridge University Press, 2012), 25–44.

> NEW MUSICK.
> *This Day is published,*
> SEI Sonate di Cambalo con Violino o Fluto
> Traverso di Felice Degiardino, Opero Terzo. Price 10 s. 6 d.
> Printed for, and sold by J. Cox, at Simpson's Musick Shop in
> Swerthing's Alley, oppofite the East Door of the Royal Exchange.
> ☞ Of whom may be had, all the above Author's Works, and
> all the newest Musick now published, all Sorts of Musical Inftru-
> ments, &c.

Illustration 3.2 Advertisement for Giardini's *Sei sonate* Op. 3. Courtesy of the British Library.
General Advertiser 16 December 1751.

agree to (7) assign and set over unto the said John Cox his Executors and Administrators the aforesaid Six Sonatas for the Harpsicord and Violin ...

Giardini does not say precisely when he relinquished his rights to Opus 3, but it is significant that whenever that transaction is discussed in the litigation it is always treated separately from the larger group of compositions that Cox was to buy from the composer in 1755.[8] Some kind of informal assignment must have taken place between October 1751 and 16 December following, on which day the newspapers announced the publication of Opus 3, this time giving its title in something like the correct form (see Illustration 3.2). The imprint 'Printed for, and sold by J. Cox, at Simpson's Musick Shop', which appears both in the advertisement and on the title-page, suggests that by then Cox was the *de facto* – if not yet the *de jure* – owner of the collection. Later, in his answer to Giardini's bill (Document 2), Cox elaborates on the nature of the deal he had struck with the composer, confirming that '(6) ... he employed Persons to engrave the said Plates and paid for the Same and for the publishing thereof at his own Expence'. Nowhere on any of the Schedules does he charge Giardini for work relating to this publication, presumably because as its proprietor he alone was responsible for all the costs of seeing it through the press and onto the market. There is perhaps no better proof of Cox's ownership of copy than the following entry in his first Schedule (A1), dated 7 May 1752:

To 1 Dozen Sonatas and Violin Case   £7 12s 6d

---

8 See below.

38 *Early collaborations*

Despite its apparent vagueness, this quite specifically bills Giardini for twelve copies of his Opus 3 Sonatas some five months after their publication. After making a sale it was useful for a music retailer, for book-keeping and stock-taking purposes, to record the name of the composer as well as the genre of the item sold; that Cox was quite scrupulous about this is apparent from other Schedule entries. However, in drawing up Giardini's account there was no need to enter the composer's name every time he bought copies of his own music; thus the many references to unattributed collections of solos, duets, sonatas and songs unquestionably relate to his Opuses 1–4.[9] Such purchases are also distinguishable from others of the same type by their cost, because Giardini acquired them from Cox at a discount of roughly 20%, paying only eight shillings each instead of the usual retail price of 10s 6d.[10]

Cox's business instincts served him well with regard to Opus 3, for the accompanied keyboard sonata became one of the most popular domestic musical media of the second half of the eighteenth century. Ronald R. Kidd considers Giardini's publication to be a 'very significant' event in the history of the genre, predating by some years the first native examples by Charles Avison, Thomas Gladwin and William Jackson.[11] The prototypes, however, were French, particularly Jean-Joseph Cassanéa de Mondonville's *Pièces de clavecin en sonates avec accompagnement de violon* Opus 3 (Paris et Lille, c.1738–40), and Jean-Philippe Rameau's *Pièces de clavecin en concerts* (Paris, 1741). During the 1750s John Walsh brought out English editions of these works, both of which Giardini purchased from Cox.[12]

Giardini's royal licence

Cox did more for Giardini than just fund the publication of his Opus 3 and allow Simpson's shop to be used as a distribution channel and sales outlet for his music; he may also have advised him on how best to avoid falling victim to the piratical activities of rival publishers, an aspect of the London book

---

9 Giardini's Opus 4, his *Sei arie* (London: John Cox, 1755), was advertised as 'Six Italian Songs'.
10 See, for instance, Schedule A1 under date 7 July 1756:
   To 6 Books of Songs   £2 8s 0d
   To 6 *Ditto* Solos   £2 8s 0d
   To 6 *Ditto* Sonatas   £2 8s 0d
   To 6 *Ditto* Duetts   £2 8s 0d
   Also, 26 November 1757:
   To 1 Book of Solos, 1 Book of Duetts, 1 Book of Sonatas and 1Book of Songs   £1 12s 0d
11 See Ronald R. Kidd, 'The emergence of chamber music with obligato [sic] keyboard in England', *Acta Musicologica* 44/1 (Jan–June 1972), 122–44, at 124; and *The Blackwell history of music in Britain 4: The eighteenth century*, ed. H. Diack Johnstone and Roger Fiske (Oxford: Blackwell, 1990), 186–88.
12 See Schedule A1 under 26 January 1753 and 29 May 1755, respectively. For a discussion of the date of Mondonville's original edition, see Bruce Gustafson and David Fuller, *A catalogue of French harpsichord music 1699–1780* (Oxford: Clarendon Press, 1990), 179.

Early collaborations 39

trade in which Cox was well versed, having had first-hand experience of it as a perpetrator. It may have been he who counselled Giardini to apply for and purchase the royal licence that prefaces his Opuses 1 and 3, thereby safeguarding the intellectual property and financial interests of both parties (see Illustration 3.3). This licence or 'privilege', sometimes also called a 'patent', was a form of copyright protection that authors of literary works occasionally acquired, and to which composers sometimes resorted in order to compensate

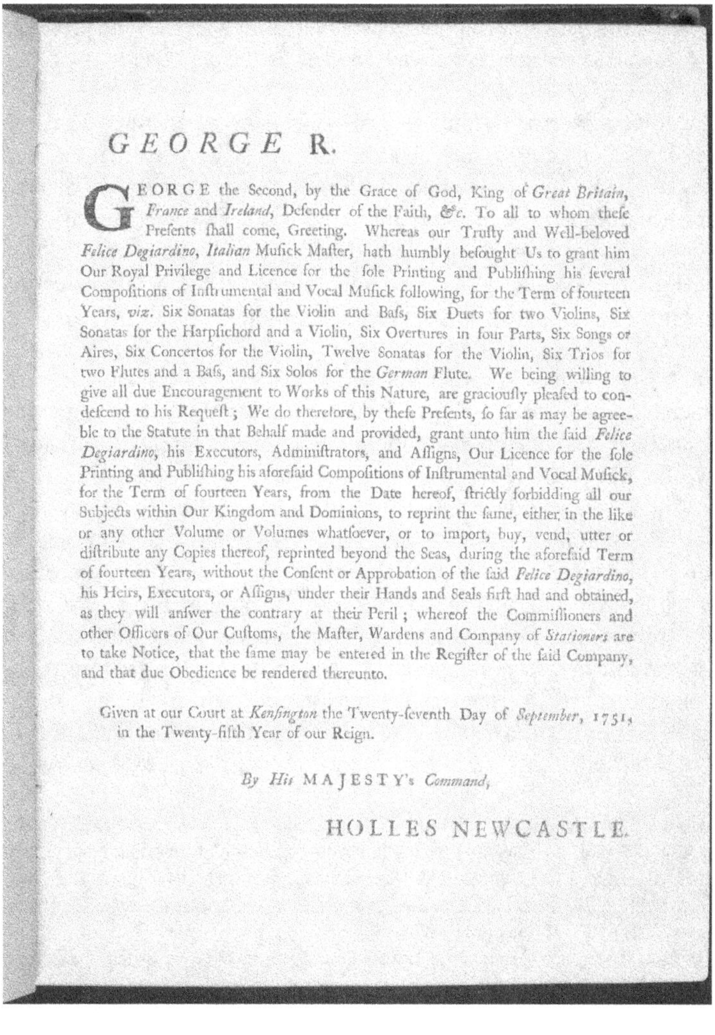

Illustration 3.3 Giardini, *Sei sonate a violino solo e basso* Op. 1. © British Library Board g.422.d.(2.).

Royal licence to print.

for the deficiencies of the 1710 Copyright Act (8 Ann., c. 19), which did not specifically deal with music.[13] Such protection did not come cheap, though at a total cost of £6 7s 6d it may have been less expensive than suffering the predations of piracy.[14] Giardini's licence, dated 27 September 1751, granted him the copyright of certain pieces for a standard term of fourteen years, and also prohibited the importation, buying, selling and distribution of copies reprinted 'beyond the Seas' without the composer's consent.[15] Most of the over forty music privileges issued during the period 1720–60 describe the compositions for which protection was sought only in the vaguest and most generalized terms, using such phrases as 'divers works' or 'several pieces of Musick'. Such haziness had certain advantages for the petitioner:

> The 'divers works' formula also made it easy to continue to use a privilege long after it had expired. Privileges were worded so that they applied only to material which was allegedly complete or well advanced at the time of the grant, but a privilege protecting 'diverse works' could be printed together with music composed years later, perhaps giving potential pirates the impression that the new publication was protected or partly protected by that privilege.[16]

Giardini's royal patent similarly refers to 'his several Compositions of Instrumental and Vocal Musick', but also specifies 'Six Sonatas for the Violin and Bass, Six Duets for two Violins, Six Sonatas for the Harpsichord and a Violin, Six Overtures in four Parts, Six Songs or Aires, Six Concertos for the Violin, Twelve Sonatas for the Violin, Six Trios for Two Flutes and a Bass, and Six Solos for the *German* Flute'. Some of these items can be identified with known Giardini publications; the first three, for instance, are clearly his Opuses 1–3, and the 'Six Songs' are presumably his *Sei arie*, Opus 4. However, it would be a mistake to imagine that every work on this list had already been composed. Although the six songs were eventually published in 1755, there is no knowing what their ontological status was in September 1751; they may have existed in manuscript, but they

---

13 Printed music was held to be within the 1710 legislation only in 1777; see Shef Rogers, 'The Use of Royal Licences for Printing in England, 1695–1760: A Bibliography', *The Library* 7th ser., 1/2 (June 2000), 133–92, and John Small, 'The development of musical copyright' in *The music trade in Georgian England*, ed. Michael Kassler (Farnham: Ashgate, 2011), 233–386, especially 270–93.
14 The costs of the licence are set out in The National Archives of Great Britain (henceforth TNA): SP 45/27, under October 1751.
15 The licence is included in the British Library copy of Opus 1 [call-mark: g.422.d. (2)] and Opus 3 [Hirsch III.225].
16 Small, 'The development of musical copyright', 284.

could equally well have been a work in progress, or even a future project as yet unrealized. Similar questions hover over the 'Six Concertos' and the 'Twelve Sonatas for the Violin': had they all been written by 1751, were they in gestation, or were they merely a twinkle in the composer's eye? Are they respectively the Opus 15 set of concertos published by Welcker in 1771–72, and the *XII Sonates à violon seul avec la basse* that appeared 'A Londre' in 1758 as Opus 6?[17] And as for the 'Six Trios for Two Flutes and a Bass' and the 'Six Solos for the *German* Flute', if they ever existed they have been lost to posterity.[18] The portfolio of Giardini's compositions listed on the privilege seems to have been a mixture of (a) pieces already composed by 1751, or very close to completion; and (b) works in popular genres, gathered in bundles of standard size, that any self-respecting composer would eventually get round to writing. By including projected as well as currently available works on the privilege, he could avoid the trouble and expense of having to procure another licence in order to protect future compositions from copyright infringement.

The Exchequer litigation provides insights into how Giardini disposed of the ownership of several other works mentioned in the privilege. On 20 June 1755, nearly four years after spending £30 on the rights to Opus 3, Cox bought the composer's Opuses 1 and 2, the *Sei arie* Opus 4 and the six overtures, also for £30 each. The date of this transaction is recorded only in Schedule A2, which enters the purchase in short form as 'Sundry Overtures and Duetts £120 0s 0d.' Although both parties naturally refer to this important agreement in some detail, the fuller and somewhat less convoluted account from Document 2 is preferred below:

> (4) ... And this Defendant [Cox] admits it to be true that the said Complainant [Giardini] in Consideration of Thirty Pounds to him in Hand paid by this Defendant (5) did agree to assign and set over unto this Defendant his Executors and Administrators the aforesaid Six Sonatas for the Harpsichord and Violin being part or parcell of the said Compositions of Vocal and Instrumental Musick mentioned in the

---

17 See *Public Advertiser* 13 January 1758. Presumably these were the same as the set of sonatas mentioned in the advertisement for 'The favourite Songs in IL DEMOFOONTE' (*Public Advertiser* 11 December 1755): '... twelve Solos, published by Subscription, composed by Sig. Degiardino, each Subscriber to pay One Guinea, upon Receipt of which is to receive three Solos, and to continue every Month till the Twelve is compleated.'

18 An additional category, 'Six Concertos for the German Flute', was inserted into the official government copy of the licence, but was subsequently dropped from the printed version; compare the latter (Illustration 3.3) with TNA: SP 44/372, 200–01. These flute concertos appear to have been yet another ghost.

said Letters Patent so granted to the said Complainant as in the said Bill (6) mentioned, ... (7) ... And that the said Complainant (8) did accordingly[,] by such Indenture of such Date and to such Purport or Effect as in the said Bill for that Purpose mentioned[,] in Consideration of the said Sum of Thirty Pounds[19] and in Consideration of the further Sum of One Hundred and Twenty Pounds therein mentioned[,] to be[,] and which really was[,] to the said Complainant in Hand paid before the Sealing (9) and Delivery of the said Indenture[,] the Receipt whereof the said Complainant did thereby acknowledge Grant sell assign and set over unto this Defendant his Executors Administrators and Assigns such part of the said Inventions or Compositions of vocal and Instrumental Musick in the said Patent contained as follows, that is to say, the (10) aforesaid Six Sonatas for the Violin and Bass, the said Six Duetts for two Violins, the said Six Sonatas for the Harpsichord and Violin, Six Overtures and Six Songs or Airs together with all the Plates thereof engraved and Copies then in the Possession of this Defendant, and all the Right, Title and Interest of the said Complainant in and to (11) the Same, To hold the said Inventions or Compositions of Vocal and Instrumental Musick Plates and Copies aforesaid, and all the Benefit and Advantage from the printing and publishing thereof to this Defendant his Executors Administrators and Assigns for the Residue of the Term of Fourteen Years mentioned in the said (12) Letters Patent, And the said Complainant did thereby for himself his Executors and Administrators covenant and agree with this Defendant ... that he the said Complainant should and would at the Expence of this Defendant ... use his ... utmost (13) Endeavours to obtain a renewall of the said Patent for a further Term of Fourteen Years for the Sole Benefitt and at the request of this Defendant ...

Two noteworthy points emerge from this passage. The Opus 3 Sonatas, which Cox had paid for back in 1751, are only now formally and legally transferred to him, along with more recently purchased items of the composer's property listed in the indenture. Also of interest is the evidence that Giardini undertook to renew the royal licence in Cox's favour, though at the latter's expense. It was unusual for a composer to take out a second privilege for himself, Francesco Geminiani, Michael Festing and John Worgan being the only examples that spring to mind; but it was just as rare for a composer to do so for the benefit of his publisher. The best known instance of this is the second royal licence granted to Handel on 31 October 1739,

---

19 Already paid for Opus 3.

Early collaborations 43

which 'authorised and appointed *John Walsh* of the Parish of *St. Mary le Strand* ... to print and publish' his works.[20] Ten years later Walsh was party to a similar agreement with the Comte de Saint-Germain, though the privilege he obtained on that occasion was not a renewal. His licence to print suggests that, like Cox, he too had purchased the rights to the composer's music: 'John Walsh, Our Musical Instrument Maker, ... hath obtained all the Instrumental *and* Vocal Musick, composed by the Count St: Germain, with a Design to engrave *and* print the same'.[21] Following these and similar precedents, Cox clearly considered Giardini's music to have such lasting appeal that a renewed licence was seen as a worthwhile investment. In the event, the composer's commitment to ensure that Cox was nominated as the rightful owner of certain pieces of his intellectual property was one he never had to fulfil, because it became a casualty of their bitter dispute over the printing of the six overtures.[22]

Subscription concerts

During the first four years of his stay in England Giardini shared the concert platform with a number of London's finest musicians. Series of weekly concerts had been an occasional feature of the capital's cultural life throughout the first half of the eighteenth century, but the format was given its greatest boost in 1750 by the failure of the Italian Opera at the King's Theatre. The season there came to a premature close at the end of April with the bankruptcy and subsequent flight abroad of the impresario Giovanni Francesco Crosa and most of his company. Following their departure, Italian opera at the King's ceased altogether and did not resume until November 1753. In the meantime, the Opera's wealthy and aristocratic devotees had perforce to seek their musical entertainment elsewhere in London's West End. Many found an outlet for their patronage at the fashionable subscription concerts, the most prestigious of which were the series held at Hickford's Room in Brewer Street, St James's, and at a more recently established venue in Dean Street, Soho. A similar situation had arisen some two decades earlier when the Royal Academy of Music, which had presented Italian opera at the King's Theatre since 1720, ran out of money after eight seasons and closed

---

20 See *George Frideric Handel: Collected documents*, ed. Donald Burrows, Helen Coffey, John Greenacombe and Anthony Hicks. 5 vols. (Cambridge: Cambridge University Press, 2013–), 3 (1734–42): 527.
21 See TNA: SP 44/372, pp. 20–21; and Comte de Saint-Germain, *Musique raisonnée selon le bon sens aux dames Angloises qui aiment le vrai goût en cet art* (London: J. Walsh, *c.*1750).
22 See Chapter 4.

its doors. To entertain the nobility over the coming winter, Lewis Granom organized a number of weekly subscription concerts at Hickford's starting on 4 January 1729. It is clear from the unusual choice of Saturday for the concerts that this series was intended to take the place of the opera.[23] The exclusive nature of the Brewer Street and Dean Street premises may be seen from the licences that concert promoters had to acquire from local justices in order to comply with 'An act for the better preventing thefts ...', and for regulating places of publick entertainment' (25 Geo. II, c. 36), the relevant sections of which came into force in December 1752. Here, for example, is an extract from the petition submitted by James Hugford, dancing master and successor to John Hickford, in October of that year:

> ... your Petitioner laid out several hundred pounds in building a large Room contiguous to his Dwelling House, for teaching his Scholars, and for Musical Performances which have been honoured with the presence of their Royal Highnesses the late Prince of Wales, the Princess Dowager of Wales, and the Duke of Cumberland, to which Room a way leads from Windmill Street, and in which there hath been for 15 years and upwards a Select Subscription Concert, composed of a great Number of the Nobility, and Persons of distinction; and to keep off all, except such, a Rule has been made, and strictly observed, to Admitt none but Subscribers, without paying a Guinea each Night at the Door[.]
>
> That your Petitioner hath sometimes Let the sai^d Room for Benefit and Subscription Concerts; but never did, nor will he Let it to any who took, or shall take, or offer to take less than five shillings at the Door[.][24]

Hickford's most recent subscription series had been those organized by Signor Palma in January–March 1749 (ten concerts) and Giuseppe Maria Manfredini in February–March 1750 (five concerts), but there was no perceptible increase in activity there after the closure of the King's Theatre; the same pattern was maintained in January 1751, when Miss Robinson

---

23 Other periods of reduced operatic activity in London, for example the seasons 1740–41 and 1744–45, also appear to have acted as a spur to concert life; see Catherine Harbor, 'The birth of the music business: public commercial concerts in London 1660–1750'. 2 vols. (Ph.D. dissertation, University of London, 2012), 2:395–96.
24 London Metropolitan Archives (henceforth LMA): WJ/SP/1752/10. 'Hugford' is a variant of 'Hickford'; see *Survey of London 31, 32: St James Westminster*, Part 2: North of Piccadilly; gen. ed. F. H. W. Sheppard (London: Athlone Press, 1963), 31:121–23. The *Survey* is cautious about attributing the building of the concert hall to John Hickford, but Hugford's licence suggests that it was indeed his family who paid for it.

initiated her ten weekly 'Musical Entertainments' supported by Michael Festing, oboist Thomas Vincent junior, 'cellist Peter Pasqualino and bassoonist John Miller.[25] No one at Hickford's appeared to notice the opportunities that were there for the taking. London's foremost concert room and the management of that venerable institution were about to experience the chill wind of competition.

Mr Ogle's series 1751–52

The gap in the market created by the temporary demise of the Opera was not properly exploited until late 1751, when Giardini and Cuthbert Ogle, a businessman with speculative instincts from the north-east of England, launched their subscription series at Dean Street.[26] Earlier that year Ogle and his wife had taken over a concert venue that was part of 'the Great-House in Thriftstreet', the Venetian ambassador's former residence in Soho, and developed the site into an opulent concert hall under the name of the Great Room, with entrances both from Frith Street and Dean Street.[27] The inaugural season was heralded in an advertising campaign of unprecedented intensity, with notices appearing in the press almost daily, sometimes in more than one newspaper. Beginning on 14 December the twenty weekly concerts were to be held on Saturdays (normally an 'opera' night), and the terms of admission and ticket prices were clearly set out in the publicity:

> The Terms of Subscription are Three Guineas for a single Ticket, and Five Guineas for a Double Ticket; the Single Ticket to admit one Person Gentleman or Lady; the Double Ticket to admit Two Gentlemen or One Gentleman and Two Ladies.[28]

Apart from hosting the series Ogle was to feature as harpsichordist, and by 26 November he had secured Giardini's services as leader and soloist. Singers such as Miss Sheward, 'La Francesina' (Elizabeth Duparc) and Galli soon signed up too, as did Vincent and Pasqualino; other performers, like bassoonists Samuel Baumgarten and John Miller, as well as some anonymous French horn players, would be booked later as programmes took shape. Ogle's target audience was at the upper end of the market, as the announcement in the *General Advertiser* for 9 December makes clear:

---

25 *General Advertiser* 26 January 1751.
26 For more on Ogle's colourful career, see Appendix 2, *s.v.* Mrs Ogle (*c.*1710–*c.*1765).
27 *General Advertiser* 21 March 1750.
28 *General Advertiser* 9 December 1751.

46 *Early collaborations*

> The Room will be disposed in the most convenient and elegant Manner for the Reception of the Company, and kept in proper Warmth, by the Help of a German Stove, to prevent them from catching Cold; and as the Proprietor is resolved to spare no Expence to make every Thing the most agreeable in his Power, he humbly hopes the Favours of the Public, being fully determined to make Additions and Improvements to their Entertainment as Occasion shall offer ...
> Attendance is given at the Room to shew it.

After his first season at Dean Street, Ogle, like Hugford, needed to obtain an 'entertainment licence' from Westminster magistrates before he could offer a second. His application, submitted and granted in the autumn of 1752, contains important generic information about the concerts, their clientele and the financial commitment involved in refurbishing and maintaining the site (see Illustration 3.4):

> That your Pet*itione*ʳ above a Year ago laid out *and* expended a very considerable Sum of Money in erecting *and* finishing in a very elegant manner a large Building for a Concert Room, for Musick and Dancing, in Danes [*sic*] Street in the said Parish of Sᵗ. Anne.
>
> That during the last Winter your Pet*itione*ʳ was honour'd with the Subscription of great Numbers of the Nobility *and* Gentry to the Concert there performed with much Approbation.
>
> And your Petitioner begs Leave to represent to this Court, that never any Disorder or the least Irregularity happen'd, nor is likely to happen at any future time, as the price of the Tickets confines the Entertainment to the better Sort of Company only.
>
> That your Pet*itione*ʳ is still greatly in Disburse [i.e. out of pocket] of the Monies laid out by him for the purpose abovesaid, And is under Covenants to pay a Yearly Rent of 160£. for a long Term yet to come.[29]

The newspapers provide valuable information about the repertoire performed during the Ogle/Giardini season in 1751–52, for they print programmes for all but the first concert. The titles and composers of vocal items, which mainly comprise operatic and oratorio extracts, are given together with the singer's name. The instrumental pieces, on the other hand, are often listed in very vague terms, as for instance '"cello concerto, Pasqualini' and 'violin solo, Giardini', leaving it in doubt whether the performers played their own or someone else's work; more specific are 'Geminiani's fourth

---

29 LMA: WJ/SP/1752/10.

Early collaborations 47

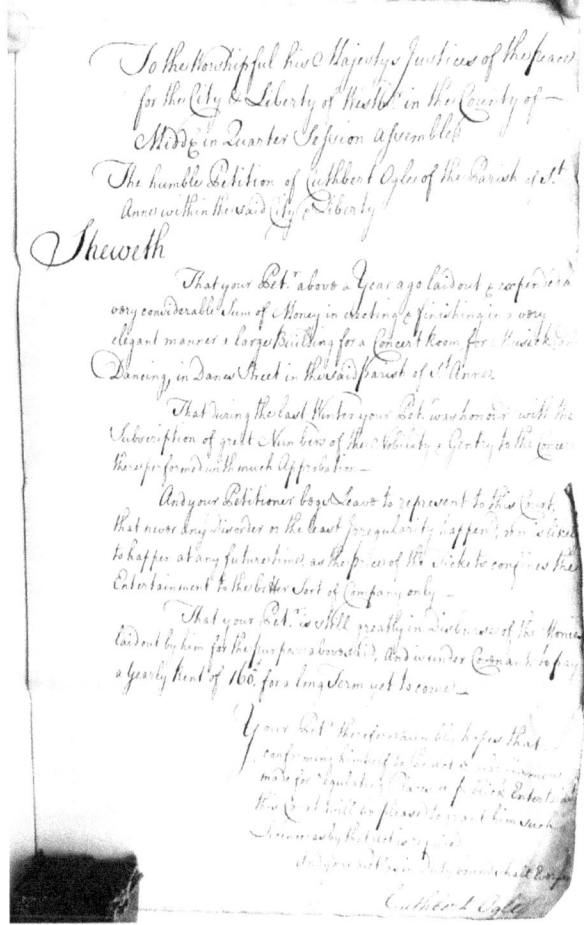

Illustration 3.4 Cuthbert Ogle's licence for the Great Room, Dean Street, 1752. Courtesy of London Metropolitan Archives City of London.

concerto' and 'Concerto for Harpsichord, Pasquali - - Mr. Ogle'.[30] As well as leading, Giardini played a concerto or solo of some description at every concert. It is impossible to say how much of his own music he included, but one can be fairly certain that on 11 January (the fifth concert) Ogle and

30 See *General Advertiser* 28 December (the third concert) and *London Daily Advertiser* 28 March (the sixteenth concert).

48 *Early collaborations*

Vincent performed one of his recently published Sonatas Opus 3; and at the sixteenth concert (28 March) the audience heard an overture and a violin duet of his composition.[31]

Giardini's influence is also noticeable in the choice of instrumental repertoire by other composers. His predilection for modern French and Italian music was apparent at the third concert when Ogle played a 'harpsichord concerto' by Rameau, perhaps from Walsh's edition (1750); and the sixth and eight concerts began with an overture by 'Sig. Conte Giulini'. Count Giorgio Giulini (1716–80) belonged to one of the noblest families in Milan; poet, lawyer and historian of his native city, he was also a dilettante composer of numerous symphonies, having in his youth taken lessons in composition from G. B. Sammartini and studied several instruments with some of the best performers in Italy.[32] As fellow members of the Milanese school sharing the same teacher, he and Giardini would have known each other well, and there can be little doubt that the latter was the channel of transmission through which Giulini's music came to England. Four concerts ended with orchestral concertos by Sammartini, probably Giovanni Battista, in which case it is likely they were taken from the set of *Six concertos in 8 parts, for violins, French horns, hoboys, &c* that Walsh published in late November 1751.[33] Of similar novelty-value, at least to London audiences, were the concertos by Charles Avison, mutual friend of Giardini and Ogle, that were included in the fourth, thirteenth, fourteenth and eighteenth concerts. The inventory of Ogle's personal effects, drawn up after his death, lists several sets of Avison concertos.[34]

It is difficult to gauge the success, financial or otherwise, of Ogle's series, but the available evidence suggests that it did not generate huge profits. Sustaining momentum over so long a period as twenty weeks was always going to be a problem, and indications are that by the fifth concert on 11 January interest was already beginning to flag. A note appended to that day's programme shows that the subscription was not yet full, and tickets on the night were being offered at half a guinea each; even by 15 February, half way through the season, tickets were available at the door and the terms of subscription were still being advertised. Even so, by the fourteenth concert Ogle was already contemplating his next series, as is clear from

---

31 The other player in the duet was Charles Froud; see *London Daily Advertiser* for that date.
32 Newell Jenkins and Bathia Churgin, *Thematic catalogue of the works of Giovanni Battista Sammartini: Orchestral and vocal music* (Cambridge, MA: Harvard University Press, 1976), 5.
33 Numbers 2 and 3 are by Hasse.
34 See John W. Molnar, 'A collection of music in colonial Virginia: The Ogle inventory', *The Musical Quarterly* 49/2 (April 1963), 150–62.

a note attached to the programme: 'The Subscribers to this Concert are requested to meet this Evening, immediately after the Concert is finished, in Mr. Ogle's House, in order to consort upon proper Regulations for next Season'.[35] A week later a new set of proposals was in place for a subscription series beginning on the last Saturday in December and continuing for twenty weeks; there were to be three classes of ticket – single (three guineas), double (five guineas) and treble (six guineas) – and subscribers who paid a deposit were to be given preference should the series be over-subscribed. Ogle lost no time in enlisting performers, and on 11 April he could announce that 'Signora FRASI is engaged for the ensuing season'.

Over the summer these ambitious plans appear to have been quietly modified, and the next we hear of a new season is on 12 December when the papers advertised another subscription, this time for a series beginning on Saturday 20 January 1753. Ogle's name is nowhere to be seen, though the venue is still Dean Street, and the number of concerts on offer is now a more realistic twelve. Giardini is not mentioned either, Signor Chabran being designated first violin with support from singers Elizabeth Turner, Gaetano Guadagni and Frasi.[36] Carlo Chabran had advanced rapidly in the public's estimation as composer and performer after arriving from Paris towards the end of 1751 or the beginning of 1752.[37] At first, Giardini, who came from the same region of north Italy as Chabran, took him under his wing and helped to kick-start his London career. However, they were soon perceived as rivals, and particularly so after an unfortunate stand-off during Miss Sheward's benefit concert at Dean Street on 17 March 1752. 'The Inspector' provides the details:

> As the Dispute that happened a few Days since at the Dean-street Concert Room, seems to have been misrepresented, I think it incumbent on me, as in some Degree concerned, to say what I know of it.
>
> Signor Giardini performed at the Benefit of Miss Sheward, (whose Merit, not any personal Acquaintance had occasioned my interesting myself for her) at my Request. Signor Chabran was engaged for Money. This Performer made Difficulties about Signor Giardini's playing after him; and it was with some Perswasion that he was at length prevailed on to let it be decided by Lots. When S. Giardini was called out to

---

35 *General Advertiser* 14 March 1752.
36 *Public Advertiser* for that date; Charles Froud (second violin), Giacobbe Cervetto ('cello), Philip Eiffert (oboe) and Miller (bassoon) joined the band later (*Public Advertiser* 23 December 1752 and 16 January 1753).
37 For more details, see Appendix 2, *s.v.* Chabran [Schabran], Charles (1723–54).

be acquainted with this, he declined the Decision; apologised to the Company for having been in some Degree the Occasion of so much Trouble about a thing of so little Consequence; voluntarily played his Solo first, and left the other in possession of the Orchestre.[38]

The rift that appears to have opened up between the two virtuosi may be traced back to this incident. Giardini must have taken his later exclusion from the Saturday concert series as something of a snub, especially on hearing of Chabran's preferment. To avoid being marginalized he somewhat belatedly joined forces with Thomas Vincent, whose family was well connected on the London musical scene; together they organized their own subscription series at Dean Street on Tuesdays (the other 'opera' night) that would run concurrently with Chabran's, to the latter's undoubted detriment.

Giardini/Vincent series 1753

The Giardini/Vincent subscription series represented something of a departure from the pattern established by Ogle. Unlike the 1751–52 series, its promotion appears to have been almost entirely removed from the public domain; proposals were never published, so we have no knowledge of ticket prices and, with the exception of the two principal players, performers are mentioned only tangentially. Information about the terms of subscription has to be gleaned from press notices dealing with other matters; and the advertisement of concert dates, apart from the first, is similarly unsystematic, as for instance when it was necessary to correct misinformation or reschedule an event. Even the number of performances is nowhere explicitly stated, and there are certainly no programmes printed in the newspapers. All these features, together with the fact that subscribers were never openly canvassed, gave the series something of the aura of a private society, supported by an exclusive network of wealthy patrons. Vincent, who had been 'Musick and Instrument Keeper to his R. H. the Prince of Wales' since April 1740, could doubtless rely on contacts in royal circles;[39] and it is likely that Mrs Fox Lane introduced Giardini to many of her aristocratic friends at an early date, for he was quickly accepted into the fashionable world of London society as both teacher and performer. According to Burney:

---

38 *London Daily Advertiser* 23 March 1752.
39 Duchy of Cornwall Archives: Household Accounts of Frederick, Prince of Wales, vol. LX (1) Warrants etc. 1738–50, p. 22 (British Library, Department of Manuscripts: microfilm 2433).

Early collaborations 51

He soon got possession of all the posts of honour in this country. He was engaged and caressed at most of the private concerts of the principal nobility, gentry, and foreign ministers.[40]

A letter from the lawyer and Handel enthusiast Thomas Harris to his sister-in-law gives us some idea of the kind of audience that attended the Giardini/Vincent series. Writing about the concert held on 27 February 1753, he says:

> I was last Tuesday evening at the concert of delitantis [*sic*] in Dean Street, where the room was entirely crowded with fine people: but they are grown so desperately refined that nothing is perfect enough for them; there was no attention given to the songs or concertos, and very far from a proper silence when Giardini played a solo: every thing [*sic*] seems to be lost in admiration of dear self and company ...[41]

The administrative structures set up to support the Giardini/Vincent concerts experienced some initial problems in the first few weeks of 1753. An announcement in the *Public Advertiser* for Wednesday 17 January, which provides the only evidence of Cox's early involvement, gives the date of the first concert as 'Tuesday next' and informs readers that:

> The Subscribers that have not received their Tickets, are desired to apply to Mr. John Cox, at the Cannon Tavern, Charing-Cross, on Friday and Saturday next, who is to attend there to receive the Remainder of the Subscriptions, and to deliver the Tickets, from Nine in the Morning till Three in the Afternoon.

However, this arrangement may not have suited Cox, for next day the same paper printed the following retraction:

> The Advertisement of Yesterday, in regard to the Delivery of the Tickets, was a Mistake; the Subscribers that have not received their Tickets, are desired to send for them to Mr. Vincent's in Shepherd Street, near Hanover-square.

---

40 Abraham Rees, *The cyclopaedia, or, universal dictionary of arts, sciences, and literature.* 39 vols. (London: Longman, Hurst, Rees, Orme & Brown, 1819–20), 16: *s.v.* 'Giardini, Felice'.
41 *Music and theatre in Handel's world: The family papers of James Harris 1732–1780*, ed. Donald Burrows and Rosemary Dunhill (Oxford: Oxford University Press, 2002), 286.

52   Early collaborations

More unwelcome publicity came with the postponement of the second concert in the series, scheduled for 30 January, which had 'to be put off for one Week, next Tuesday being the Martyrdom of King Charles the First'.[42] The series organizers had been aware of this problem since the beginning of the year, for the newspaper advertisement announcing the date of the first concert (23 January) notes that 'The second Day's Concert is to be on the Monday following, Tuesday being the Martyrdom of Charles the First'.[43] Evidently the Dean Street management, who generally resisted performers' attempts to dictate the concert schedule (see below with regard to Violante Vestris), would not countenance such a change. There also appears to have been a problem with heavy traffic outside the first concert, and the disorderly conduct that followed prompted the organizers, who were doubtless fearful of breaching the terms of the venue's licence, to issue the following reminder:

> The Subscribers to Signor GIARDINI and Mr. VINCENT's Concert in Dean-street, are desired to order their Coaches to Thrift-street, with their Horses-Heads to the Square, and the Chairs to Dean-street, to prevent any Accidents that may happen from the Unruliness of the Coachmen and Chairmen as was found the last Night; though strict Orders was given them to come to the different Doors abovementioned.[44]

Despite these teething troubles the series grew in popularity, and by the end of February its organizers had to announce that access to the concerts would in future be restricted, implying that the subscription was full:

> THE Subscribers to Sig. *Giardini* and Mr. *Vincent*'s Concert, in Dean-street, Soho, having found great Inconveniency in bringing their Friends who are not Subscribers, on paying Half a Guinea; it's hoped, that no Person will take it ill, that they cannot be admitted for the future. The Subscribers own Tickets admit one Person, either Gentleman or Lady, the Red Tickets admit Ladies only.[45]

---

42 *London Daily Advertiser* 26 January 1753. Almost immediately after his execution on 30 January 1649 Charles was portrayed as a martyr; from 1662 to 1859 a special service for that date was annexed to the Book of Common Prayer by royal mandate, and the anniversary was required to be kept as a day of national fasting. One's credentials as a good Whig or Tory were in part measured by one's attitude to the martyr.
43 *Daily Advertiser* 4 January 1753.
44 *Public Advertiser* 31 January 1753. 'Thrift' (now 'Frith') Street led towards Soho Square. Another minor hiccup was the postponement of the concert arranged for Tuesday 17 April to the 24th, because of Holy Week; see *Public Advertiser* 16 April 1753.
45 *Public Advertiser* 27 February 1753.

Meanwhile, on 20 January, Chabran's Saturday series at the same venue got off to an equally auspicious start, if the papers are to be believed:

> Last Saturday was performed the first Night of the Subscription Concerts, at the Great Room in Dean-street, Soho, to a numerous and brilliant Audience, all of whom expressed great Satisfaction with the whole Performance, in particular with the celebrated Sig. Chabran, who met with universal Applause.[46]

> The celebrated Sig. Chabran, who met with such extraordinary Applause last Saturday Night at the Subscription Concert in Dean-Street, Soho, will this Evening play a Solo on the Violin at the same Place, being the second Night of the above Concert.[47]

Once both series were up and running, the critics lost no time in comparing the respective merits of the main protagonists. According to 'The Inspector':

> There was a Time when the Elegance of S. Giardini prevailed against the Execution of S. Chabran, amazing as it is: But the latter has of late made a Point of it, to adapt his Performance to the Taste of those before whom he is to play; and 'tis fitting he should be told the Consequence. 'Twas the Opinion of all who heard him on Saturday, that whatsoever he had declin'd in the surprising, he had gained in the pleasing; and what he had dropp'd in the Execution, he had obtain'd in Tone.[48]

No account of the Giardini/Vincent series would be complete without mentioning the part played in it by Violante Vestris. A member of the famous French family of dancers and musicians of Italian extraction, she arrived from Paris in December 1752, having earlier appeared in the programmes of the Concert Spirituel as the singer of certain unspecified Italian songs.[49] Her purpose in coming to London was possibly to join the line-up of soloists that Giardini had recruited for the forthcoming season, and he quickly fell victim to her charms. However, his attempts to promote her career by inserting her into an already packed concert schedule created a situation that was to strain relations

---

46 *Public Advertiser* 22 January 1753.
47 *Daily Advertiser* 27 January 1753.
48 *London Daily Advertiser* 26 January 1753.
49 Gaston Capon, *Les Vestris: Le "diou" de la danse et sa famille, 1730–1808, d'après des rapports de police et des documents inédits* (Paris: Mercure de France, 1908), 52; Constant Pierre, *Histoire du concert spirituel 1725–1790* (Paris: Société française de Musicologie, 2000), 263. For her earlier career, see John A. Rice, 'Mid-eighteenth-century opera seria evoked in a print by Marc'Antonio dal Re', *Music in Art*, 34 (Spring–Fall 2009), 153–64.

with his collaborators to breaking point. This mini 'soap opera' played itself out in a series of press releases issued by the parties concerned in late March and early April 1753. The trouble began when Giardini arranged a benefit for Violante at Dean Street on 27 March, offering his services as first violin and Cox's as ticket agent.[50] All this was done without the knowledge or consent of Mrs Ogle, who by then was managing the venue; what is more, the date of the proposed benefit was a Tuesday. Giardini subsequently asked Mrs Ogle to move the subscription concert to Monday, doubtless to avoid clashing with the Vestris engagement, though this is never explicitly stated. For various reasons, including the fact that Chabran had already arranged a benefit at Dean Street on Monday 26 March, Mrs Ogle felt she could not oblige Giardini on this occasion, and so three days before the concert was due to take place the public were informed that the advertisement regarding Vestris's benefit was a mistake, the date and venue therein mentioned having already been booked for one of the Giardini/Vincent subscription concerts, which would now proceed as planned.[51] Vestris's benefit was hastily re-scheduled for 12 April at the Little Theatre in the Haymarket, where she was joined by Vincent and Giardini, the latter playing a solo and a concerto.[52] Giardini made known his displeasure at Mrs Ogle's perceived intransigence by announcing that his participation in her forthcoming Dean Street benefit on Saturday 14 April could no longer be guaranteed:

> SIGNOR DE Giardino thinks it his Duty to inform the Publick, that he is not under any Contract or Engagement to play at the Concert in Dean-Street, Soho, for the Benefit of Mrs. Ogle; and that the Advertisement handed about on that Account is without his Consent.[53]

This represented a serious escalation of their dispute, for the agreement securing Dean Street as the venue for the Tuesday series had stipulated that Giardini and his orchestra should perform at Mrs Ogle's benefit. She clearly considered his refusal to play to be a breach of trust, if not of contract, and responded accordingly:

> Whereas Sig. Giardini has thought proper to inform the Public, that he is not obliged by any Contract, to perform at my Concert, it is my Duty to acquaint them that he is so far engaged to perform at my Benefit, as being undoubtedly included in his own Band, it being one of the Conditions of their having the Room, that the whole Band should

---

50 *London Daily Advertiser* 16 March 1753.
51 *Public Advertiser* 24, 26 and 27 March 1753.
52 *Daily Advertiser* 5–7 and 9–12 April 1753.
53 *Daily Advertiser* 5 April 1753; repeated on the following two days.

Early collaborations 55

perform Gratis for my Benefit, to which Condition Mr. Vincent, as the acting Manager, engaged for Sig. Giardini, himself, and the Band. For the Truth of this I appeal to Mr. Vincent.[54]

Fences may have been mended by 12 April, for the advertisement for Mrs Ogle's benefit printed by the *Public Advertiser* assumes that the performers will be: 'First Violin, by Sig. Giardini; Hautboy, Mr. Vincent; the Vocal Part by Signora Frasi, and others; the other Instrumental Performers the same as the Tuesday Night Concerts'. The same newspaper also included a brief statement from Giardini agreeing to play, which would have been fine had he left it at that:

> SIGNOR GIARDINI has this Day consented to perform at Mrs Ogle's Benefit, on Saturday next, with Mr. Vincent and their whole Band.
> Note, Signor Giardini's refusing to play was owing to some Misunderstanding between him and Mr. Vincent.[55]

The appended 'Note', apportioning some of the blame for the dispute to Vincent, was enough to rouse the latter's ire, and on the very day of the concert he sought to put the record straight:

> MR. Vincent declares that Sig. Giardini's refusing to play at Mrs. Ogle's Benefit was not owing to any Misunderstanding between him and Sig. Giardini, but with Mrs. Ogle, as he has declared, on Account of her refusing him to change one of the Nights of his Subscription Concert from Tuesday to a Monday, which Mrs. Ogle had promised to a Person of Distinction, not to have any such Thing of a Monday; and that his complying at last to perform for her, is owing to Mr. Vincent telling him on Tuesday Night at Dean-street, before several Persons of Quality, his Verbal promise to him for performing, and his fixing the Time to the latter End of March or the Beginning of April, and to stay untill Sig. Frasi and Sig. Vestris's Benefit was over. This Mr. Vincent is ready, if there should be Occasion at any Time, to declare upon Oath.[56]

---

54 *Public Advertiser* 7 April 1753.
55 *Daily Advertiser* 12 April 1753; for different wording, see *Public Advertiser* for the same date.
56 *Public Advertiser* 14 April 1753; Frasi's benefit at the Little Haymarket on 2 April consisted of a performance of Handel's *Acis and Galatea*, which Giardini led.

Vestris, Giardini and Vincent *did* perform at Mrs Ogle's benefit that day, together with Frasi, Galli, Pasqualino and Miller; but the atmosphere must have been decidedly frosty.

In his first answer to the Exchequer bill (Document 2), John Cox sheds light on the part he played in the administration of the three subscription series that Giardini organized at Dean Street between 1753 and 1755:

> (53) ... And this Defendant [Cox] saith that he was appointed Treasurer and Manager by the said Complainant [Giardini] and on his behalf to all such Concerts (54) and did receive the Profitts and paid the Expences thereof[,] save only that as to the last of the said Concerts the said Complainant did himself receive All his share of the Subscription Money for the Concert[,] no part of which he ever paid over to this Defendant.

His testimony is invaluable because it contains information about the finances and organization of the concerts that is to be found nowhere else; just occasionally, however, what he has to say is a little perplexing. With regard to the 1753 series, we learn from Cox's answer to the amended bill (Document 5) that he went by coach from Sweeting's Alley to Dean Street for '... 15 Nights Attendances at Mr Degiardinos and Mr Vincents Subscription Concerts as Inspector and Manager' (Schedule B1). So far as one can tell, however, there were not fifteen concerts in the series; between the date of the first (23 January) and what was almost certainly the last (24 April) there were only fourteen Tuesdays, and that number includes the two days when there were no concerts (30 January and 17 April). To make Cox's journeys to the West End tally with the number he claimed for, one would need to include the day he and Giardini had set aside for settling up their accounts (19 April), as well as the benefits for Signora Vestris and Mrs Ogle (12 and 14 April), though these hardly qualify as Giardini/Vincent subscription concerts. According to Cox's first answer:

> (54) ... the whole Profitts of the said Subscription Concert (55) ... did amount to the Sum of Three Hundred [and] Seventy one Pounds Fourteen shillings or thereabouts[,] after Payment of all Expences in Respect thereof

The principal performers, it seems, had agreed to split the profits evenly, for when Cox accounted with Giardini he paid him a half-share, that is £185 17s, for which he took a written receipt. In today's terms, this sum is roughly equivalent to £21,685.[57]

---

57 See www.nationalarchives.gov.uk/currency/.

Giardini/Chabran series 1754

Despite glowing reviews, Chabran's first series of Saturday concerts appears to have been no more successful than Ogle's, a situation in large measure attributable to the Giardini/Vincent series running parallel with it on Tuesdays. Another factor was the series of six 'Spiritual Concerts' instituted by the violinist Giuseppe Passerini and his wife Christina (soprano), who arrived from Edinburgh in February 1753 hoping to establish themselves in London 'in case that they meet herein with sufficient Encouragement'.[58] Their concerts, organized in conjunction with the oboe-playing Plà brothers, took place at Dean Street on Thursdays. With so much musical activity to choose from – apart from the three subscription series, numerous benefits and other charity events were available in the capital – it is hardly surprising that the market quickly became saturated, and the inevitable consequence of competition for such a niche audience was a drop in demand. For Chabran, the effects of over-supply were felt as early as the first concert when he was forced to admit non-subscribers and offer financial inducements:

> Ladies and Gentlemen will be admitted at Half a Guinea each; any of whom chusing to become Subscribers after the Concert, the Half Guinea to be allowed in Part of Payment for their Tickets.[59]

This initiative did little to stimulate sales, and by the sixth concert take-up was still slow. The Passerinis, too, were adversely affected by the glut; after warning the public to subscribe before their first concert on 15 March, 'because after that Day no Subscriptions will be taken in', they added the following note to that day's advertisement: 'Tickets to be had at the Concert Room at half a Guinea each for the Pit, and 5s. for the Gallery'.[60]

Chabran, however, was undeterred by returns below expectation, and even before his series had run its full course he was planning another, as is evident from the advertisement for the penultimate concert, which informed the public that 'The Subscription Book is opened for the ensuing Season. The First Violin by Sig. Chabran'.[61] As we have seen with Ogle's plans for a second season, an invitation to subscribers, though suggestive, is not proof positive that the mooted series actually went ahead, and any doubts that modern scholars might have had about the existence of a 1754 season at Dean Street have only been reinforced by the lack of relevant references in the Burney newspapers. However, that lack is more apparent than real, for

---

58 *Public Advertiser* 27 February 1753.
59 *London Daily Advertiser* 20 January 1753.
60 *Public Advertiser* 7 and 15 March 1753.
61 *Public Advertiser* 31 March 1753.

58 Early collaborations

a search of other databases which plug gaps in the Burney collection amply demonstrates that the series did indeed take place, if not quite as originally envisaged. On 17 December 1753, the *Daily Advertiser* carried the following notice giving details of the forthcoming season (Illustration 3.5):

> SIG. DEGIARDINO and CHABRAN's SUBSCRIPTION CONCERT, at the Great Room in Dean-Street, Soho, begins on Monday the 7th of January next, and will continue every Monday till the ten Concerts are completed.
> Tickets to be delivered, at Three Guineas each, at Signor Degiardino's, in Cork-Street, Burlington-Gardens; at Signor Chabran's; In Little St. John's Street, Golden-Square; and at Simpson's Musick-Shop in Sweeting's Alley, Royal Exchange.
> The Infirumental Parts by Signor Degiardino and Signor Chabran, &c. the Hautboys by Signor Plà's; Violoncello, Signor Lanzetti; Vocal Parts by Signora Degiardino and Signora Chabran.
> Note, No Tickets will be delivered after Monday the 31st inftant.

Illustration 3.5 Advertisement for the Giardini/Chabran subscription series. Courtesy of the Library of Congress.
Daily Advertiser 17 December 1753.

Instead of assuming the mantle of 'The First Violin', Chabran was now to share that role with Giardini, though the priority given to the latter's name in newspaper advertisements suggests that their relationship was less than equal. Compared with the opaqueness of the marketing strategy used for the Giardini/Vincent series, there is now greater focus and transparency in the way concerts are publicized and managed; their number is specified, programmes are advertised in advance and subscribers receive precise information about performers, prices, tickets and how to acquire them. Subscriptions at three guineas, admitting the bearer only, and five guineas, admitting the subscriber and two ladies, could be purchased from the organizers' lodgings or Simpson's music shop. The list of supporting musicians included the singers Signora Chabran and Vestris (now 'Signora Degiardino'), as well as the 'cellist Salvatore Lanzetti and the Plà brothers.[62] The only administrative hitch appears to have been the postponement by a week of the first concert, originally planned for 7 January.

According to the *Daily Advertiser*, the ten concerts took place on 14, 21 and 28 January; 4, 11, 18 and 25 February; and 4, 11 and 18 March 1754.[63] The day was changed to Monday so as not to compete for audiences with

---

62 John Miller joined the ensemble later.
63 These dates should be added to Simon McVeigh's otherwise very useful *Calendar of London concerts 1750–1800* at http://research.gold.ac.uk/10342/.

the King's Theatre where, since the previous November, Italian opera had resumed on Tuesdays and Saturdays. The concerts consisted of the customary two 'Acts', the first beginning with an overture, usually by either Chabran or Giardini, and finishing with a concerto by Geminiani; in between were songs from the women and concertos from the men. In Part 2 a concerto for bassoon and a Corelli concerto invariably book-ended a mixture of songs, trios and instrumental solos. Exchequer Document 2 informs us that the 1754 subscription series generated '(56) ... the Sum of One Hundred and Forty Pounds or thereabouts[,] after payment of all Expences in Respect thereto'. On 29 March Cox accounted with Chabran and Giardini who, on receipt of £70 each, signed and executed a release to Cox bearing that day's date. Mrs Ogle claimed her charge for hire of the Great Room by staging a benefit on 4 April at which the musicians who took part in the series played – presumably for nothing.

The Giardini/Chabran series was not the only one presented at Dean Street that season. In early December 1753 the Passerinis called for subscriptions for a twelve-concert series commencing initially on Thursday 10 January, but later deferred for a week 'by Reason most of the Subscribers are not yet come to Town'.[64] Two guineas bought twelve tickets, and three guineas twenty-four; tickets were also available on the night at five shillings. The vocal parts were performed by Catherine Fourmantel, Signora Passerini and others, who undertook to sing 'every Night some of the Italian and English favourite Songs of Mr. Handel'; Giuseppe Passerini led the band, which included three instrumentalists who also played for the Monday series, namely Lanzetti and the Plà brothers. The Passerini series, however, cannot have made much money; the sixth concert on 21 February was put off till further notice because the room was double-booked, but the remainder appear to have been abandoned for commercial reasons. A series of twelve concerts was an over-optimistic assessment of the market's potential, as the advance publicity for Signora Passerini's benefit on 1 April admits:

> The remaining seven Subscription Concerts of Sig. Passerini are put off on Account of the many Diversions which are in Town on the Thursdays; but the first Concert will be in April, and the others will continue Weekly till the whole are compleated: if some of the Subscribers should not be in Town in the Time that the said Concerts will be, Sig. Passerini is ready to return the Subscription Money.[65]

---

64 *Public Advertiser* 8 December 1753 and 10 January 1754.
65 *Public Advertiser* 27 February 1754.

60 *Early collaborations*

A later version of the same advertisement informed subscribers that they could use their tickets to gain admittance to the benefit, and that 'the Sixth Subscription Concert of Sigr Passerini's, will be in Easter Week'.[66] There is, however, no evidence that the sixth or indeed any of the remaining concerts in the series ever took place.

Giardini/Frasi series 1755

Any hopes that Giardini might have had of repeating the success of the 1754 season in a follow-up series with Chabran would have been dashed by news of the latter's death later that year. In his search for a new collaborator, Giardini needed to find someone who was popular with London audiences and yet available for the upcoming season, and the person that appeared to match those criteria best was the soprano Giulia Frasi. In England since 1742 when she joined the Middlesex opera company at the King's Theatre, Frasi later became a soloist for Handel's oratorios, and her 'sweet and clear voice, and a smooth and chaste style of singing' made her a great favourite with the public.[67] She and Giardini knew each other well, having worked together many times, most recently in York in August 1754. In the following January the papers announced that their subscription series would begin at Dean Street on Monday the 13th instant; double and single tickets, at five and three guineas respectively, were available from each of their lodgings and Simpson's music shop. So far as other advertising is concerned, Giardini appears to have reverted to the same arcane methods that he employed in his series with Vincent, namely, minimal publicity and a total lack of published programmes. Information about the number of concerts and the names of the supporting performers is similarly lacking, though a note appended to the initial advertisements states: 'In order to oblige the Subscribers of the above Concert, Mrs. [*sic*] Vanneschi has given Signora Curioni (one of the Opera Singers) Leave to sing'.[68] In a similar spirit of co-operation Giardini and Frasi put off the concert they had planned

---

66 *Public Advertiser* 19 March 1754. The original date and venue for the Passerinis' benefit – Dean Street on 1 April – was later changed to the King's Theatre on 2 April; this led to an very public spat between the couple and Frasi, who had booked the theatre for a benefit performance of Handel's *Samson* on that day; see *Public Advertiser* 29 March–2 April 1754 for the exchanges. She later re-scheduled to 25 April with a performance of *L'Allegro, il Penseroso ed il Moderato*, which Giardini led.

67 Charles Burney, *A general history of music from the earliest ages to the present period*. 4 vols. (London: for the author, 1776–89), 4:449.

68 *Public Advertiser* 11 and 13 January 1755; Francesco Vanneschi was then manager/impresario of the King's Theatre.

for Monday 17 March, because it clashed with the benefit in support of 'Decay'd Musicians, or their Families' at the King's Theatre, a gesture that enabled Frasi to sing for that charitable cause. From the press advertisement re-scheduling the postponed concert to 31 March we learn that it was the ninth in the series, and 'that the Three Nights which are to come (exclusive of this) will be continued every Monday till the Whole are compleated'.[69]

The greater involvement of King's Theatre personnel in these concerts was probably a consequence of Giardini's appointment as leader of the Opera orchestra for the 1754–55 season. Curioni joined Frasi in singing at his Dean Street benefit on 10 March 1755, but Regina Mingotti, the Opera's leading lady who had also been booked, cried off at the last minute: 'Signora Mingotti, who design'd to have favour'd the Benefit with her Performance, is prevented by Illness, not being able to perform at the Opera on Saturday last.'[70] Mingotti withdrew from subsequent engagements until she had recovered, and Frasi had to deputize for her in Galuppi's *Ricimero* on the following Saturday (15th) and the Tuesday after that (18th). On Wednesdays and Fridays in Lent, though not during Holy Week, Frasi also sang at Covent Garden in certain of Handel's oratorios – *Samson* and *Joseph and his brethren*, and probably *Judas Maccabaeus*, *The Choice of Hercules* and *Theodora*. Giardini, on the other hand, played for Thomas Augustine Arne's rival series at Drury Lane, comprising two performances of *Abel* (Friday 14 and 21 March) and one of *Alfred* (Wednesday the 19th instant). When Frasi had her benefit at Dean Street on 20 March Giardini returned the compliment and performed for her, along with Guadagni. Their participation in Pasqualino's benefit on 24 April may have been a similar *quid pro quo*, perhaps acknowledging his contribution to their subscription series.

With regard to the finances of the Giardini/Frasi concerts, Cox states in Document 2 that, unlike in previous years:

> (65) ... the said Complainant [Giardini] never paid to this Defendant the Subscription Money by him[,] the said Complainant[,] received on Account of the said Concert ... (66) ... \save only that this Defendant did receive some Money that was taken each night at the Door of the Concert Room, All which this Defendant disbursed towards payment of the Band of Musick employed at such Concert[.] And the said Complainant's Share of the Moneys so taken at the Door was not Sufficient to pay and satisfye his proportion of the Expence of such

---

69 *Public Advertiser* 29 March 1755.
70 *Daily Advertiser* 10 March 1755.

Band of Musicks[,] but the Remainder thereof was paid by the said Complainant himself/[.]

Cox re-affirms this position in his further answer (Document 4), adding:

(40) ... that he settled an Account of that Concert with the said Complainant when it appeared that there was a Ballance resting in this Defendant's Hands on Account (41) of that Concert amounting in the whole to the Sum of Sixty three pounds Nine Shillings and no more[,] being the part or Share of Giulia Frasi ... of the profitts of that Concert[,] the said Complainant (42) having himself received more than his Share thereof ... And thereupon this Defendant did by the Direction of the said Complainant pay the said Sum of Sixty three pounds Nine Shillings to the said (43) Giulia Frasi [,] and she gave a Receipt to this Defendant for the Same in full for all Moneys received by this Defendant on Account of that Concert, the said Complainant having himself received his part or Share of such Profitts ...

The admission of non-subscribers to the concerts suggests that the series was not well attended, and it appears that even the money taken at the door did not amount to much. Having noted the number of patrons and read the financial runes, Mrs Ogle may well have concluded that she would be better off charging Giardini and Frasi for the hire of the hall, instead of doing what she had done in previous years and taking a benefit at which he and his associates appeared gratis.[71] This extra cost could have been another factor in reducing the dividends to a level below those achieved in 1753 and 1754. Certainly, the rank and file musicians had to wait quite some time for their money. In Document 4 Cox claimed that Giardini

(12) ... did sometime about the latter End of the Year One Thousand seven Hundred and Fifty five give this Defendant a Note of his[,] the said Complainants[,] under his Hand for the Sum of One Hundred [and] Eighty One Pounds Thirteen Shillings or thereabouts (13) which was so given without this Defendant's paying any Consideration for the Same, and was so given only in Order that this Defendant might shew the Same to the Band of Musick then employed in the last Subscription Concert mentioned ... to let (14) them see that the said Complainant had given this Defendant such Note out of which they might be paid the said Complainant's Share of the Moneys due for their Performance at such Concert ...

---

71 Her only benefit in 1755 was on 25 February when Ms Fourmantel, Guadagni and the violinist Giovanni Battista Marella performed.

Cox's complicity in this ruse enabled Giardini to keep the band members at bay for some ten months after the season had finished. Then on 5 March 1756 the following notice appeared in the *Public Advertiser*:

> The Musicians who performed last Year at Mr. Giardini and Signora Frasi's Concert in Dean-street Great Room, that have any Demands on Account of the said Concert, are desired to call on Mr. Giardini at his Lodgings in Pall-mall this Day and To-morrow, from Ten in the Morning to Two in the Afternoon.

Little wonder that the 1755 series was Giardini's last for several years.

Giardini and the Opera 1756–57

Cox was of assistance to Giardini not only as treasurer for the various concert series discussed above, but also as an administrator when he and Mingotti took over management of the King's Theatre in 1756–57. The previous two years at the Opera had been turbulent to say the least, with Vanneschi the impresario and Mingotti the diva at loggerheads on a range of financial and policy issues; by the summer of 1756, after a campaign of mutual vilification waged via the newspapers and various pamphlets, it was obvious that their working relationship had broken down irreparably.[72] However, two lawsuits against Vanneschi that came to judgment around this time presented Mingotti with an escape from what seemed like an impossible situation. At Easter 1755 the dancer Charles Lalauze successfully sued Vanneschi in King's Bench for £100 and £130; a year later the impresario disappeared from the scene, possibly taking refuge on the Continent because he could not meet his legal obligations in London.[73] With her adversary out of contention, Mingotti assumed the role of manager of the Opera for the 1756–57 season with the support of Giardini and several influential backers, including Mrs Fox Lane.[74] Writing some thirty-five years later, the Irish

---

72 See Michael Burden, *Regina Mingotti: Diva and impresario at the King's Theatre, London*. Royal Musical Association Monographs 22 (Farnham: Ashgate, 2013), Chapter 2: 'Mingotti in London, 1754–57', particularly 64–81.
73 TNA: KB 168/14 (Entry Book of Judgments: Trin 1752–Easter 1756) Easter 1755, 9. Burney (*General history* 4:467) states that Vanneschi was committed to the Fleet, but there is no evidence of his confinement there or in any other gaol; see TNA: PRIS 4/2 and PRIS 10/89; 10/134; and 10/180.
74 According to a correspondent of Elizabeth Harris, '[Mingotti] sings every Wednesday at Mrs Lanes'; see the letter dated 11 March 1755 in Burrows and Dunhill, *Music and theatre*, 303–04.

impresario Robert Bray O'Reilly recalled the lengths to which Harriet went to secure the King's Theatre for her clients:

> In the year 1756, Lady Bingley and other admirers of the Opera, being desirous to place that entertainment under the direction of Mingotti and Giardini, applied to Mr. Crawford for the House. This he declined letting, assuring her Ladyship that he was only acting as an Agent, and adding, that under such circumstances, he could not surrender the management to any person without a perfect assurance of their responsibility for the payment of the rent and Performers. The Duke of Grafton, the then Lord Chamberlain, upon Mr. Crawford's stating the circumstances to him, approved of his conduct, and desired, "that he might assure Lady Bingley if ever the Opera House should be lett to persons not of a respectable description, he would refuse his Majesty's licence, and prevent the performance of Operas." Lady Bingley made personal application to the Lord Chamberlain to no purpose; nor could she succeed until the Duke of Marlborough undertook to be security for the rent, performers, and all incidental expences; and the licence was in consequence granted to *his Grace* for that season.[75]

The endeavours of Mingotti and Giardini, however, proved financially unsuccessful and ended with them, in Burney's words:

> ... acquiring, for a while, the sovereignty in the opera kingdom, by which gratification of ambition they were soon brought to the brink of ruin, as others had been before them. ...
>
> But though great applause was acquired, and appearances were favourable, yet the profits to the managers were so far from solid, that

---

75 *An authentic narrative of the principal circumstances relating to the opera-house in the Hay-Market; from its origin to the present period* (London, 1791), 7. Peter Crawford was then treasurer of the Opera at the King's Theatre. Burden suggests that it was William Augustus, Duke of Cumberland, who provided the main financial backing for the Opera that season, a view he claims is supported by Horace Walpole's correspondence; see *Regina Mingotti*, 54. In fact, neither Walpole himself nor his editors make such an assertion: see *The Yale edition of Horace Walpole's correspondence*. 48 vols. (New Haven, CT: Yale University Press, 1937–1983), 20:557. Burden connects Walpole's statement that 'Mars is turned impresario' with Cumberland's military exploits, but that sentence could as easily apply to Marlborough who had just been made Master-General of the Ordnance, an appointment that brought him into prominence at the beginning of the Seven Years' War in 1756. It is also worth pointing out that Elizabeth, Duchess of Marlborough, was a pupil of Giardini's and the dedicatee of his *Sei arie* Opus 4, which Cox published in 1755; see William Thomas Parke, *Musical memoirs*. 2 vols. (London, 1830), 1:51.

Early collaborations 65

they found themselves involved at the end of the season in such difficulties, that they were glad to resign their short-lived honours, and shrink into a private station.[76]

In Document 5 of the Exchequer litigation, Cox states that Giardini undertook to pay him £30 if he attended the five operas produced at the King's Theatre that season and assisted with their administration.[77] Giardini flatly denied this, and so to substantiate his claim Cox lists, in the second of the document's two Schedules (B2), the dates and titles of the operas at which he presented himself at Giardini's behest. These included performances of the pasticcio *Alessandro nell'Indie*, Hasse's *Il re pastore*, Nicola Conforto's *Antigono*, Giardini's *Rosmira* and Galuppi's *Euristeo*:

> The Second Schedule to which the above Written Answer Refers[.]
> A Particular Account of this Defendants Attendances on the behalf of the said Complainant at the five several Operas Performed in the Hay Markett for which Attendances the Complainant Promised to pay this Defendant thirty pounds[.]

1756 December	11th	1st Night of	Alessandro Nell['] Indie
	14th	2d Night of	Ditto
	18th	3d Night of	Ditto
	21st	4th Night of	Ditto
1757 January	4th	5th Night of	Ditto
	8th	6th Night of	Ditto
	11th	7th Night of	Ditto
	15th	8th Night of	Ditto
	18th	1st Night of	Ill [sic] Re Pastore
	22d	2d Night of	Ditto
	25th	3d Night of	Ditto
	29th	4th Night of	Ditto
February	1st	5th Night of	Ditto
	5th	6th Night of	Ditto
	8th	7th Night of	Ditto
	12th	8th Night of	Ditto
	15th	9th Night of	Ditto
	19th	10th Night of	Ditto
	22d	11th Night of	Ditto
	26th	12th Night of	Ditto
March	1st	9th Night of	Alessandro &c
	5th	10th Night of	Ditto
	8th	1st Night of	Antigono
	12th	2d Night of	Ditto
	15th	3d Night of	Ditto

(*Continued*)

---

76 *General history*, 4:467–68.
77 For a detailed account of his duties, see Chapter 4, p. 76.

66 Early collaborations

(*Continued*)
[*second column*]

March	19th	4th Night of	Ditto
	22d	5th Night of	Ditto
	26th	6th Night of	Ditto
	29th	7th Night of	Ditto
April	2d	8th Night of	Ditto
	16th	9th Night of	Ditto
	19th	10th Night of	Ditto
	23d	11th Night of	Ditto
	26th	13th Night of	Ill Re Pastore
	30th	1st Night of	Rosmira
May	3d	2d Night of	Ditto
	7th	3d Night of	Ditto
	10th	14th Night of	Ill Re Pastore
	14th	4th Night of	Rosmira
	17th	5th Night of	Ditto
	21st	6th Night of	Ditto
	24th	15th Night of	Ill Re Pastore
	31st	1st Night of	Euristeo
June	4th	2d Night of	Ditto
	7th	3d Night of	Ditto
	11th	4th Night of	Ditto
	14th	5th Night of	Ditto

These five Operas were performed at the Kings Theatre in the Haymarkett the Season above mentioned forty seven Nights and at which this Defendant Attended as Inspector and Manager for and on the behalf of the Complainant and at his request[.]

An additional performance of *Rosmira*, given on Saturday 18 June 1757 for the benefit of the Marine Society, was no concern of Cox's and is therefore omitted from this list.[78] The above schedule corrects errors made by more recent attempts to compile the same information. Perhaps the most egregious of these mistakes appears in *The London Stage*, which states that the work performed on 24 May was *Rosmira*; the advertisements in the London press agree with Cox that it was in fact *Il re pastore*.[79]

---

78 The Marine Society, the world's first public maritime charity, was set up at the beginning of the Seven Years' War to clothe and equip men and boys for service at sea. The King's Theatre benefit raised £59 6s; see *A list of the subscribers to the Marine Society, from June 1756 to September 30th, 1759*, 3, in Jonas Hanway, *An account of the Marine Society* (London, 1759).
79 Cf. Burney, *General history*, 4: 467; *The London stage 1600–1800: Part 4, 1747–1776*, ed. George Winchester Stone Jr. 3 vols. (Carbondale: Southern Illinois University Press, 1962), 2:601; and Burden, *Regina Mingotti*, 120–21. According to Professor Burden there were forty-nine operatic performances that season, but one can only arrive at this figure by counting the concert for the benefit of 'Decay'd Musicians' held at the King's Theatre on 24 March; see *Regina Mingotti*, 11.

4 Giardini and Cox in court

Giardini cannot have been surprised when Cox's lawyers served process upon him early in 1758; after all, he had amassed a large number of debts that remained outstanding, and his creditor was a man with whom he had had a major disagreement over the costs of printing his overtures.[1] A network of well-connected friends and patrons doubtless rallied round to provide moral and financial support and facilitate access to the best legal advice. Significantly, the lawyer who signed his Exchequer bill was George Nares, brother of James Nares, one of the organists and composers of the Chapel Royal, and formerly organist of York Minster;[2] and the attorney who represented Giardini at the King's Bench hearing was one John Lane, possibly a relation of Mrs Fox Lane. Nevertheless, for a foreign national living in London the prospect of doing battle in an English court of law must have been daunting.

Giardini's indebtedness to Cox

After introducing us formally to the parties and their attorneys, the King's Bench litigation announces that 'Felice Giardini ... late of Westminster in the County of Middlesex Gentleman was Attached to Answer unto John Cox in a Plea of Trespass on the Case'. Normally one would have instituted bill proceedings when prosecuting such an action at common law, but process by original writ was also possible, and contemporary legal practice books advised plaintiffs to choose this option if the damages sought were over fifty pounds. Giardini must have ignored the first summons to appear – probably

---

1 See below.
2 George later became a distinguished judge; see *Oxford dictionary of national biography*, *s.v.* Nares, Sir George (1716–1786). For Giardini's connection with James Nares, see above, Chapter 2, pp. 14 and 18.

at Hilary 1758 – for which contempt of court Cox was able to sue out a writ of attachment against him. According to this, Giardini's attendance at the start of the Easter term would have been secured either by monetary pledges or the seizure of some of his possessions, which would have been forfeit had he defaulted. The preamble also states that Cox's plea was of the type known as 'trespass on the case', that is, an action instituted for the recovery of damages caused by an injury inflicted without the use of force, or where the damages sustained were consequential only. He complained that Giardini was indebted to him not only in several sums of money, but also for unpaid goods and services provided over a period of about six years. The composer's monetary debts, the first of which he incurred shortly after arriving in London, had accumulated through a series of promissory notes written on the following dates in 1751: on 9 July for £20; on 21 September for £21; on 2 November for £28 9s 0d; and on 3 December for twelve guineas. In the following year, he borrowed a further six guineas on 25 February; and on 2 July and 10 December 1753 Cox lent him £21 and £20 respectively on the strength of similar notes of hand.

Having enumerated the extent of Giardini's cash debts, Cox turns his attention to less tangible matters and to the 'diverse Goods Wares and Merchandizes by the said John before that time Sold and delivered to the said Felice at his special Instance and request'. This part of the document presents the plaintiff's case as a series of 'alternative' pleas, to each of which is attached a claim for £1000.[3] These include claims for 'so much money as he therefor [sic] reasonably deserved to have'; 'for Work and Labour Care and diligence ... before that time done performed and bestowed ... in and about the Business of the said Felice'; 'for Money ... lent and advanced'; 'for Money laid out Expended and paid to the said Felice'; and 'for Money by the said Felice before that time had and received to the Use of the said John'. These claims are of course largely fictional, the legal equivalent of taking aim with a blunderbuss in the hope that some buckshot will hit the target. Matters had apparently come to a head on 1 January 1758 when the parties accounted together and discovered that Giardini owed £211 19s 8d in respect of the various claims. Since then the latter had refused to settle his debts, though frequently requested to do so by Cox, 'to the said John his Damage of Two Hundred and Thirty Pounds And therefore he brings his Suit etc.'

---

3 Alternative pleading permitted a party in a court action to allege two or more independent claims or defences, so that, should any of the claims or defences be held invalid or insufficient, the others would still have to be answered.

In an attempt to frustrate the King's Bench proceedings, Giardini put into practice the old adage that attack is the best form of defence and counter-sued Cox on the equity side of the Court of Exchequer in the following term, that is, Trinity 1758. Although given to prolixity, Giardini's bill and Cox's various answers add substance to the somewhat vague and formulaic language of the latter's common-law suit, and delineate clearly the three main areas of dispute between the parties, namely: (a) Cox's allegedly disastrous printing of Giardini's 'Six Overtures'; (b) the charges for the administrative duties that Cox performed at Giardini's subscription concerts and at the Opera house; and (c) the state of Giardini's account at Cox's music shop, which was in arrears and included the several promissory notes mentioned in the King's Bench litigation.[4] Welcome as the discovery of this new material is, it is not without its problems of interpretation: the amount of documentation is colossal; the evidence is at times contradictory; and there can be little doubt that Giardini's recollection of events is confused over dates, and that Cox is occasionally economical with the truth. However, even in the matter about which their perceptions diverge most radically – the circumstances surrounding the publication of the overtures – it has been possible to piece together a narrative that accounts for most, if not all, of the verifiable facts.

The publication of Giardini's Overtures

Giardini's bill begins by setting out the background to that part of his complaint that deals with Cox's publication of his 'Six Overtures'; what follows covers some of the ground already discussed in Chapter 3, though from Giardini's perspective. His testimony (Document 1) confirms that on 27 September 1751 he was granted a royal licence or privilege for the sole printing and publishing of a number of his compositions for a period of fourteen years, and suggests that within the next couple of months he sold to Cox the rights of one of these works – his 'Six Sonatas for Harpsichord and Violin' – for £30.[5] On 20 June 1755 Cox also bought Giardini's 'Six Sonatas for Violin and Bass', his 'Six Duets for Two Violins', the 'Six Overtures', and his 'Six Songs or Airs', all for a further £120.[6] The composer transferred to Cox all his right, title and interest in these works, and '(11) ... all

---

4 The matter of Giardini's account at Cox's shop is discussed in Chapter 5.
5 The sale must have taken place before 16 December 1751, when Cox published Giardini's *Sei sonate di cembalo con violino o flauto traverso*, Op. 3.
6 *Sei sonate a violino solo e basso*, Op. 1; *Sei duetti a due violini*, Op. 2; *Sei arie*, Op. 4. The anomalous position that the 'Six Overtures' occupy in the Giardini catalogue is discussed below.

the Benefit Profit and (12) Advantage which might arise from the printing and publishing thereof ... for the residue of the said Term of fourteen Years'. As part of the agreement Cox was to present Giardini with twelve sets of each of the four last-mentioned collections, and deliver to him an additional one hundred copies of the 'Six Overtures' by the end of November 1755, for which he would receive £105 four months later. Some of the repertoire that Giardini signed away was in the form of engraved plates, but all the overtures were still in manuscript and Cox undertook to have these engraved.

However, Giardini claimed that the proofs of the 'Six Overtures' that Cox subsequently sent him for inspection were '(16) ... extreamly incorrect and improperly engraved', and so he forthwith 'applyed himself to Seignor Pasquali *and* desired him to correct *and* Amend the sai^d proof Sett'.[7] Pasquali duly obliged, and Giardini returned the corrected proofs with instructions to make the necessary changes and print off one hundred copies as per the agreement. Allegedly, it took Cox until March or April 1756 to produce just twenty-five corrected copies,[8] which on examination Giardini claimed were as faulty as the first set of proofs. The prints were consequently deemed to be '(20) ... of little or no value[,] neither coud your Orator [i.e. Giardini] sell or dispose thereof'. He complained to Cox about the poor quality of the workmanship, which he demonstrated by procuring:

> (21) ... several eminent professors of Musick to meet at [his] House to endeavour to play the said Six Overtures from the Volumes so printed and delivered by the said John Cox ... and after spending much time in such their Endeavour the said professors (22) declared it was impossible to play the Six Overtures from the said printed Books Notwithstanding they had frequently played the said Overtures from the manuscript Copies of your Orator.

Forced to acknowledge the publication's shortcomings, Cox apparently persuaded Giardini to correct some of the Overtures in order to make a second edition that was '(24) ... equal in Goodness to the original Composition thereof', and that would do justice to works that the composer claimed 'had been played by several Eminent Professors as well in England as in parts beyond the Seas with universal Applause'. Cox then produced yet another

---

7 The double bass player Francis Pasquali was the younger brother of violinist Niccolo. Both may have come to England in the early 1740s. According to Trevor Fawcett, Niccolo was in Norwich in 1741 and 1743; see his *Music in eighteenth-century Norwich and Norfolk* (Norwich: Centre for East Anglian Studies, 1979), 6.

8 Changed from twenty by an interlineation.

set of about twenty copies of the Overtures in the following May or June, but again, despite the many corrections made by Giardini, they were found to be wholly defective, and '(26) ... coud not be corrected so as to be rendered useful without great Labour and expence and loss of time'. Giardini therefore denies that he owes £105 for one hundred copies of the 'Six Overtures', because Cox did not deliver a single one that was fit for purpose. He insists that when 'several Persons of great Rank and Dignity' requested copies of the print, he had to correct the parts (presumably by hand), at great trouble and loss of time to himself; and by revealing that he had been criticized by '(42) ... eminent Professors of Musick for suffering such incorrect engraving to come into the world under your Orators name', he appears to be staking a claim for what lawyers today would call 'reputational damage'. He also suggests that he suffered loss of earnings because, had Cox carried out the work properly and delivered the Overtures on or before 30 November 1755, '(44) ... many persons of Rank and Distinction then in the Town for the Winter Season' would have bought them for 'a very considerable Sum of Money and for not less than two hundred Guineas profit'. Giardini concludes his bill by asking for a subpoena to secure Cox's appearance in court to answer his complaint, and an injunction to block the King's Bench suit.

Cox's side of the story is encapsulated in Documents 2, 4 and 5, and the sequence of events set out below is a conflation of all three records and the Schedules appended thereto. He begins his defence by denying Giardini's claim that he delayed delivering the Overtures until March or April 1756, and that the copies were incorrectly engraved and unserviceable. His recollection of events is as follows. On receipt of Giardini's plates and the Overtures still in manuscript, Cox took the latter to John Phillips of Broad Street, Soho, and '(Document 2: 20) ... Signor Frances Pasquali of the same place Engravers', to have them engraved, because Pasquali was the person usually employed by Giardini for that purpose. He then sent the new plates to 'John Gramiant' of Water Lane, Fleet Street, who printed just '(21) ... one Volume or Sett of the said Overtures' as a first proof.[9] About 1 October 1755 Grumeant took this copy to Giardini for inspection, and both he and Pasquali, who was present at the time, agreed it '(24) ... to be Correct and Right'. Grumeant was therefore instructed to proceed with the printing of the hundred copies, which he did under Pasquali's supervision, and these were

---

9 See entries on Schedule A1 dated August and September 1755, which refer to the 'Carriage of Proofs'. The printer John Grumeant/Grameant, was formerly of Off Alley, St Martin's in the Fields, and later of King's Street, St Anne's, Westminster. He was incarcerated for debt in the King's Bench Prison, whence he applied for relief in December 1778; see Ian Maxted, *The London book trades, 1775–1800: A preliminary checklist of members* (Folkestone: Dawson, 1977), 97.

delivered to Giardini's lodgings in Pall Mall by 28 November following. Cox then ordered another fifty for himself to sell, but only after the completion of that order did the composer claim that the hundred he had received were defective. Both parties agreed that the print should be checked against the manuscript, and when Pasquali and Giardini collated the two sources they found that '(32) ... the plates were properly engraved according to the said Manuscript but (33) that the said Manuscript was Incorrect, and that was the Reason of the said One Hundred Setts or Volumes delivered to [Giardini] were Incorrect and Improper'. Giardini thereupon set about correcting the manuscript, and Pasquali amended the plates under his direction and figured the bass. Cox paid the latter £2 for doing all this, and for '(34) ... attending the said John Gramiant in the reprinting part of the said Overtures', which cost an additional £5 in paper and other overheads. One hundred copies of the amended overtures were then run off, and on or about 9 March 1756 Giardini took receipt of them and gave them his approval. Cox denies that Giardini convened a gathering of 'Eminent Professors of Musick' to play through the overtures in order to demonstrate the inadequacies of the printing; that persons of quality had requested copies; that Giardini had been censured for allowing inaccurate copies to circulate under his name; and that he had been put to any trouble correcting them. He adds that sometime later, when he called on the composer to collect payment, he was asked to wait for his money because Giardini had sent fifty of the hundred copies 'abroad' and had not yet been reimbursed.

Giardini's 'Six Overtures' are something of a musicological conundrum, since no collection by him with that title, printed or in manuscript, has survived. The one that comes closest in terms of date and content is the *Four overtures & one quattro compos'd by Sig.^{r} Felice Degiardino and one concerto with two violins & two hautboys obligato compos'd by Sig.^{r} Gio Batta Sr Martini*, which was 'Printed for J^{no} Cox'.[10] Published sets of overtures by different composers usually came in sixes; sets of overtures by the same composer could appear in collections of six (for instance, those by Ciampi and Greene), eight (Arne, Giuseppe Sammartini) or twelve (Boyce, Niccolo Pasquali). The collocation of pieces in different genres by different composers that one finds in the *Four overtures* [etc.] is anomalous, and suggests that the contents were brought together hastily in response to the

---

10 Re-issued by Robert Bremner as *Five overtures composed by Sig^r Felice Giardini and a grand concerto by Sig^r Gio: Battista St Martini* (c.1765). The concerto is No. 73 in Newell Jenkins and Bathia Churgin, *Thematic catalogue of the works of Giovanni Battista Sammartini: Orchestral and vocal music* (Cambridge, MA: Harvard University Press, 1976), 97.

exigencies of a particular situation. The newspapers first refer to the collection not in an advertisement with the legend '*This Day is published*', commonly used to announce the publication of a new work, but in a barely noticeable footnote to the much larger advertisement for Mingotti's favourite songs from Jommelli's *Demofoonte*, which appeared in the *Public Advertiser* for 11 December 1755.[11] This states that the 'Four Overtures and one Quattro, composed by Sig. Degiardino, and one Concerto, with two Violins and two Hautboys Obligato, composed by Sig. Geo. Batta St. Martini' were 'to be had at the abovementioned Places', namely Giardini's lodgings in Pall Mall, Mr King's in Brook Street, and Simpson's music shop, but it is not made clear if the collection was 'available' or merely 'forthcoming'. The date of this advertisement is significant, for it comes less than a fortnight after Cox first delivered a hundred copies of the 'Six Overtures' to Giardini, which for one reason or another were deemed inaccurate and unsuitable for sale. This suggests that between 28 November and 11 December 1755 a decision was made to re-brand the 'Six Overtures' as *Four overtures* etc. Although the title-page of the latter collection does not give the date of publication, a press advertisement indicates that it first appeared on 18 March 1756.[12] This is near enough to the date on which Cox sent Giardini the amended copies of the 'Six Overtures' (9 March 1756) to suggest that the two collections are in fact one and the same.

If the *Four overtures* is a revamped version of the 'Six Overtures', under what circumstances did the transformation of the latter into the former become necessary? In answering that question I should like to propose the following scenario. We know from the litigation that, when the copies produced by Cox in November 1755 were rejected, both parties agreed to correct and reprint only some of the overtures. Had Giardini wished to correct them all, he no doubt could have done so, but such an undertaking might have entailed a considerable delay, and the risk of missing the beginning of the winter season, which he regarded as a lucrative retail opportunity, may have been too great. The problem required immediate attention, and Giardini struck on what he thought was a quick fix – replacing the worst of the engraved pieces with two of a more straightforward nature, which he had to hand and could give the engraver perhaps in neatly copied exemplars. The announcement regarding the *Four overtures* appended to the

---

11 See also *Public Advertiser* for the following day and 2 January 1756; the advertisement reproduced in Michael Burden, *Regina Mingotti: Diva and impresario at the King's Theatre, London*. Royal Musical Association Monographs 22 (Farnham: Ashgate, 2013), 80 is from the latter issue not that of 11 December, as the caption claims. Smaller notices advertising the *Demofoonte* songs only appeared on 10 December.
12 *Public Advertiser* for that date.

Mingotti 'favourite Songs' advertisement was left deliberately ambiguous in the hope that Cox would expedite matters, but in the event it took him another three months to complete the work, much to Giardini's exasperation, no doubt. When the parties litigated two years later, the 'Six Overtures' was retained as the title of the collection in dispute for simplicity's sake, and because that was how it appeared on Giardini's licence, from which he quotes extensively at the beginning of his bill.[13]

When the overtures finally saw the light they were dedicated to 'the Hon[BLE] Harriott Lane by her most Oblig'd and Very Hum[ble] Servant Felice Degiardino'.[14] As his most supportive patron it may have been Giardini's wish to present her with a copy of the work, and it is easy to understand why he should have wanted it to be accurate. On the other hand, he ought perhaps to have realized sooner that Cox did not operate to the most exacting standards, a fact that would have been evident as early as 1751 from his publication of the Opus 3 Sonatas; that collection contains a large number of mistakes, though not so many as Giardini sourly claimed on the title-page of a later French edition, which appeared 'Revuë et Corrigée de 554 Fautes'.[15] Knowing that Cox was not the most careful worker, and for the avoidance of error, it was perhaps incumbent on the composer to provide him with better copy.

Cox's administration of concerts and operas

As we have seen in Chapter 3, Cox's testimony contains invaluable data about the subscription money and box-office receipts for the series of concerts that took place in 1753–55, and how the profits arising therefrom were apportioned. It is clear from Document 1 (26–28) that Giardini had appointed Cox 'Treasurer' for those three seasons, and in Documents 2 and 4 the latter

---

13 Bremner's re-issue of Giardini's *Sei sonate* Opus 1 (*c*.1765) advertises the availability of the composer's '*Six overtures* Opus 4'; this was shorthand for the collection that Bremner re-named *Five overtures composed by Sig[r] Felice Giardini and a grand concerto by Sig[r] Gio: Battista S[t] Martini* (*c*.1765), which was itself a re-issue of the *Four overtures & one quattro... [etc.]*.

14 For a reproduction of the decorative title-page, see Gerald Gifford, *A descriptive catalogue of the music collection at Burghley House, Stamford* (Aldershot: Ashgate, 2001), 86. Its engraver – the printer and publisher Thomas Cobb – had connections with the Simpson family; see *New Grove Dictionary of music and musicians*. 29 vols. (2nd edn, London: Macmillan, 2001), 23:411, *s.v.* 'Simpson, John'.

15 While in Paris in October 1756, Giardini acquired the French equivalent of the British 'royal licence to print' – the 'Privilège du Roy' or 'Privilège Général'; he then had his Opuses 1–3 re-engraved to produce Parisian editions of the same, despite having sold the rights to Cox.

describes himself as both 'Treasurer and Manager', responsible for receiving the takings and paying the concert expenses. However, Giardini was unhappy that Cox appeared to charge him an administration fee of £42, arguing that, if this was in order, it should have been paid not just by him but by the other three performers too. In Document 5 Cox explains that Giardini '(17) … is indebted to him this Defendant in the sum of forty two Pounds for his Attendance at Sundry times (18) as Inspector and Manager but not as Treasurer of such Subscription Concerts'. He insists that the charge is payable by Giardini alone, and not by his collaborators, because they each appointed someone else to inspect and take account for them. Cox claims that he was employed solely by Giardini, his '(29) … said Attendances having been at the desire and by the Order and on the behalf of the said Complainant'. Giardini had repeatedly protested that he had not been told how this additional expense had come about, so at the end of Document 5 Cox provided the necessary information in the first of two Schedules (B1) dated 2 February 1759:

The First Schedule to which the Above written Answer refers[.]

A Particular Account of this Defendants Charge on the Complainant for this Defendants Attendances *etc* as Inspector and Manager on behalf of the said Complainant in Relation to the Subscription Concerts in the Complainants Bill particularly mentioned[.]

		£	s	d
1753	To 15 Nights Attendances at Mr Degiardinos and Mr Vincents Subscription Concerts as Inspector and Manager for Mr Degiardino from the Royal Exchange to Dean Street Concert Room at £1. 1s. 0d Pe^r Night and \ for/ Coach hire £1. 1s. 0[d]	16	16	0
1754	To 10 Nights Attendances at Mr Degiardinos and Mr Schabrans Subscription Concerts as Inspector and Manager for Mr Degiardino from the Royal Exchange to Dean Street Concert Room at £1. 1s. 0[d] Pe^r Night and Coach hire £1. 1s. 0[d]	11	11	0
1755	To 12 Nights Attendances at Mr Degiardinos and Signora Frasi's Subscription Concerts as Inspector and Manager for Mr Degiardino from the Royal Exchange to Dean Street Concert Room at £1. 1s. 0[d] Pe^r Night and Coach hire £1. 1s. 0[d]	13	13	0
		£42	0	0

From this, it is apparent that Cox charged a guinea a night for his attendance, plus one guinea per series for coach hire to and from the West End and his home in the City.

76 Giardini and Cox in court

Cox also alleges in Document 5 that he is owed money for attending performances at the King's Theatre during the 1756–57 season, when Giardini and Mingotti were in charge.[16] He states that he was present at '(31) ... the five several Operas performed in the Haymarkett forty seven (32) Nights ... at the Request and upon the Account of the said Complainant'.[17] Although no fee had been agreed for his services, Cox claims that at the end of the season, which had not been a success financially, Giardini promised to pay him £30, acknowledging that such a sum was poor recompense for all his efforts. To make amends Giardini swore that if the Opera house remained under his control in 1757–58, he would appoint Cox treasurer in place of the then incumbent Peter Crawford and pay him Crawford's salary, estimated at £100 per annum. In the circumstances, Cox believes that '(42) ... the two several sums of forty two Pounds and thirty pounds are just and reasonable'. To justify the £30 charge, Cox gives an outline of his duties at the King's Theatre at the time. He was employed '(37) ... to take care that the Door keepers did not admit any Person or Persons But those who had Ticketts or paid their Moneys at the time of Entrance'. Each night he was '(38) ... to take ... an Account of the number of tickets received by the several Doorkeepers and Boxkeepers and ... compare the number of ticketts with the moneys or Cash taken by them respectively'. Cox also had to check '(38) ... to see (39) if such Ticketts did agree with the Number of Ticketts returned and also to take a Copy of Each Nights Expences attending the said Performance at the Opera aforesaid and of the Profits arising therefrom And to Enter such Accounts in a Book kept by the Complainant for that Purpose at his the Complainants (40) House which this Defendant regularly did'. On several occasions he visited Giardini in his lodgings and elsewhere to help him settle the accounts with Crawford, '(40) ... for (41) which Attendances this Defendant never made any Charge on the Complainant or received any satisfaction whatsoever of him for the same'.

---

16 See the last entry under 26 November 1757 in Schedule A1.
17 See Chapter 3, pp. 65–66, where the operas performed that season are listed.

5 Giardini's account at Cox's music shop

Of central importance to this study is the first of the two Schedules (A1) that Cox included as part of his answer (Document 2) to Giardini's unamended bill. Such lists and inventories, which have been described as 'pure gold dust' on account of the detailed nature of their material, have in the past produced rich pickings for historians, literary scholars, musicologists and the like.[1] A1 is not only the most extensive of the four Schedules submitted by the defence; it is also the most significant from an evidential point of view, being a transcript of the ledger in which Cox recorded the business he transacted with Giardini over the years.[2] If the Schedule is what it purports to be – an honest account of Giardini's expenditure on goods and services at the Simpson/Cox music shop between July 1751 and February 1758 – then there must inevitably be some connection between the debits entered therein and his multifarious musical activities during the same period. However, finding that connection has not always been straightforward. Some of Cox's charges are described in terms so brief and cryptic as to be virtually impenetrable, and others do not appear to relate to anything Giardini was doing at the time, so far as our current knowledge of his biography takes us; a certain amount of speculation has therefore been applied to such cases in order to make sense of them. The interpretation of the vast

---

1 Judith Milhous and Robert D. Hume, 'Eighteenth-century equity lawsuits in the Court of Exchequer as a source for historical research', *Historical Research* 70 (June 1997), 231–46, at 233. See also Curtis Price, Judith Milhous and Robert D. Hume, *The impresario's Ten Commandments: Continental recruitment for Italian opera in London 1763–64*. Royal Musical Association Monographs 6. (London, 1992); and Cheryll Duncan and David Mateer, 'An innocent abroad? Caterina Galli's finances in new Handel documents', *Journal of the American Musicological Society* 64/3 (Fall 2011), 495–526, which make extensive use of Chancery and Exchequer schedules, respectively.
2 Cox refers to this book in his further answer (Document 4, lines 27–32), and states that he allowed Giardini to peruse it before taking him to court.

majority of entries, however, is unproblematic and consistent with what we know of Giardini's contemporary activity as a teacher, concert promoter and performer. For ease of presentation, information extracted from the Schedule has been organized under the following headings, some of which may overlap: violin costs, Giardini's other instruments, music purchases, other expenses, advertising costs, and Giardini's picture. Single items of interest are discussed in the footnotes to the Schedule itself.

Violin costs

One of the most intriguing aspects of the document is what it tells us about Giardini as a customer of Cox's shop: the purchases he made – including music, instruments and their accessories – and the services he bought. A number of entries relate to his spending on replacement parts for violins that were probably the property either of his fellow professionals or students, or were destined to be sold on. Some of these costs were doubtless minor repairs and adjustments arising from everyday 'wear and tear', as well as essential items such as new strings. Of greater interest are the disbursements on various procedures, summarized below, that were carried out with the intention of modifying the design or set-up of the instrument:

Year	Part	Quantity	Cost
1751	New neck	1	@ £1 1s 0d (including fingerboard)
	Bridge	2	@ 6d
1752	New belly, i.e. top of the instrument	3	@ £1 5s 0d
	New fingerboard	2	@ 5s 0d
	New neck & fingerboard	2	
1753	New neck	5	
	Bridge	2	
1754	New neck	1	

The radical nature of these alterations – replacing soundboards, necks, bridges and fingerboards – would have had the effect of significantly enhancing the tonal quality of the instruments, and anyone wishing to emulate Giardini's tone and technique would have considered them prerequisites. Such changes reflected both a general trend in contemporary musical taste and advances in the violin's technical capabilities. As concert venues and audiences became larger, so too did the need to produce a bigger sound. More sound meant greater string tension, which increased the pressure on the bridge and the instrument; this could have caused the belly to collapse, and may explain why Cox had to replace three of them, longer and thicker

bass bars and more substantial sound-posts presumably being fitted at the same time. In response to a fairly widespread rise in pitch and the demands for increased volume, the violin bridge was gradually modified from the flatter, thicker variety into the thinner, higher and more steeply curved form. The increase in its height necessitated a corresponding raising of the fingerboard so that it might more easily follow the angle of the strings. Up to about the middle of the eighteenth century the neck of the violin, seen in profile, had emerged in a more or less straight line from the body, and the fingerboard was elevated to meet the strings by means of a wedge inserted between it and the neck. Raising the bridge would have required a still thicker wedge and consequently a thicker neck, but this would have had an adverse effect on contemporary developments in violin technique, which called for a thinner neck to afford the player greater left-hand agility and enable the extension of the instrument's compass of stopped notes through shifting. The wedge was therefore discarded altogether and a thinner, longer neck employed, tilted back at a steeper angle in order to achieve the necessary tension. The fingerboard was also lengthened, thus facilitating high position-work, and its camber increased in keeping with the curvature of the bridge.

These changes were part of a process that began around the mid-century and saw most of the original instruments from the 'Golden Age' of violin making ($c.1690$ to $c.1750$), including virtually all the great eighteenth-century instruments, rebuilt to meet the demands of composers and players of the day for increased power and a greatly extended compass. Cox's account of Giardini's expenditure on replacement parts for his violins is redolent with implications. These alterations were a sign of the times, the violin's set-up being changed to satisfy a refined and expanding technique, a desire for increased *cantabile*, and a need for greater volume to fill larger concert venues and enable the soloist in a concerto to compete with the bigger orchestra of the later eighteenth century. According to recent research, these developments in the fittings of the violin took place gradually over a substantial period of transition between $c.1760$ and $c.1830$.[3] The costs that Giardini incurred in 'modernizing' the instruments of pupils and professional colleagues constitute some of the earliest evidence we have for that process, which appears to have begun, at least in England, a decade earlier than hitherto imagined.

---

3 Robin Stowell, *Violin technique and performance practice in the late eighteenth and early nineteenth centuries* (Cambridge: Cambridge University Press, 1985), 26; Robin Stowell, *The early violin and viola: A practical guide* (Cambridge: Cambridge University Press, 2001), 33.

Unsurprisingly, several entries on Schedule A1 record the purchase of violin strings. These are frequently described as 'ring strings', a term commonly found in contemporary newspaper notices advertising violin accessories.[4] However, the precise meaning of 'ring' in this context is obscure. It is has been suggested that a 'ring string' was one that was covered, that is, overspun with metal, but entries such as the following indicate that the term is more likely to denote a coiled length (hence 'ring') of string:

	£	s	d
To 6 Rings of 1st	0	3	0
To 21 Rings of 1st and 2d Strings	0	10	6

In mid-eighteenth-century England the violin's E and A strings – and the D for that matter – were made solely of gut. The only covered string in use at the time was the G, which was wound with silver or copper wire to improve its speaking properties and give it greater tonal brilliance; this is evident from Schedule entries such as 'To 4 Rings Silver 4th £0 4s 0d'. From this and similar entries we can calculate that the G string cost a shilling and the other three were sixpence each; a set of strings could be bought for 2s 4d, that is, at a discount of tuppence.

Giardini's other instruments

Although Giardini was first and foremost a violinist, Thomas Mortimer's *Universal Director* (1763), which covered London and its environs, lists him as a teacher of singing and the harpsichord as well as a composer.[5] This is not surprising, since eighteenth-century musicians were expected to teach a variety of domestic instruments; indeed, as Peter Holman has pointed out, '[p]rofessionals ... had to be able to play any exotic instruments their aristocratic pupils wished to learn'.[6] We know from contemporary newspapers that a music master hoping to attract new students usually advertised his proficiency on a range of instruments; this was especially so outside London, where limited demand made it difficult for teachers specializing in

---

4 See, for instance, the reference to John Simpson's advertisement in Chapter 2, footnote 64.
5 'An eighteenth-century directory of London musicians', *Galpin Society Journal* 2 (March 1949), 27–31.
6 Peter Holman, *Life after death: The viola da gamba in Britain from Purcell to Dolmetsch* (Woodbridge: Boydell Press, 2010), 163; see also Simon McVeigh, 'Italian violinists in eighteenth-century London' in *The eighteenth-century diaspora of Italian music and musicians*, ed. Reinhard Strohm (Turnhout: Brepols, 2001), 139–76.

only one or two instruments to earn a living.[7] The fact that Giardini wrote pedagogical works on the harpsichord, violin and violoncello indicates that he was as susceptible to market forces as his fellow musicians. Evidence possibly relating to his teaching of conventional instruments such as these appears in certain entries on Schedules A1 and A2; for instance, on 22 January 1752 he bought a 'Double Harpsichord' from Cox for £42, presumably to replace the old instrument he had traded in two days earlier for £20; and on 2 January 1754 he acquired a 'cello and a bow for ten guineas, which Cox bought back from him at the same price three years later, doubtless after he had finished giving some pupil or other a course of lessons. Some of Giardini's other purchases, however, are suggestive of even greater versatility as a teacher. In January 1756 Cox sold him 'a Manderlean' for a couple of guineas; if this was a mandolin it was presumably the Neapolitan type of instrument, with four courses of strings tuned in fifths $g–d'–a'–e''$ and with which a violinist would have been entirely comfortable, even though it was played with a plectrum.[8]

More significant for Giardini's compositional output was the 'guittar', that is the 'English guittar', for which he paid Cox one guinea in November 1753.[9] A member of the cittern family, the guittar – also known as the 'cetra', 'citera', 'cittra', and even 'cuter' – was cheap, elegant and relatively easy to play, qualities that doubtless account for its tremendous vogue in Britain in the second half of the eighteenth century. John Frederick Hintz, a Moravian furniture- and instrument-maker living in London, claimed in 1755 to have been its inventor and to have taught it for years, but the first professional

---

7 Richard D. Leppert, 'Music teachers of upper-class amateur musicians in eighteenth-century England' in *Music in the classic period: Essays in honor of Barry S. Brook*, ed. Allan W. Atlas (New York: Pendragon Press, 1985), 133–58.
8 Some authors have labelled this instrument the 'mandoline'; see James Tyler and Paul Sparks, *The early mandolin* (Oxford: Clarendon Press, 1989), chs. 6–8. Paul Sparks updates their study in 'The mandolin in Britain, 1750–1800', *Early Music* 46/1 (May 2018), 55–66. The mandolin became popular in Britain from the mid-1750s onwards partly through the performances of touring virtuosi like Gabriele Leoni (Leoné) and Giovanni Battista Gervasio, who both wrote a *Méthode* for it. Leoni may have been in London as early as 1758 as a participant in Ann Ford's concerts; see Holman, *Life after death*, 158–59, 237. When Giardini became impresario at the King's Theatre for the second time in 1763, he employed Leoni to recruit opera singers in Italy; see Price, Milhous and Hume, *The impresario's Ten Commandments* for an account of their subsequent falling-out.
9 See also Schedule A1 under date 29 May 1755. Studies of the guitar include Philip Coggin, '"This Easy and Agreable Instrument': A history of the English guittar', *Early Music* 15/2 (May 1987), 205–18; Peter Holman, *Life after death*, especially Chapter 4; Panagiotis Poulopoulos, 'The guittar in the British Isles, 1750–1810'. (Ph.D. dissertation, University of Edinburgh, 2011); Matthew Spring, 'Benjamin Milgrove, the musical 'Toy man', and the 'guittar' in Bath 1757–1790', *Early Music* 41/2 (May 2013), 317–29.

musician to offer lessons on the instrument was the organist Thomas Call, who advertised his services from 2 March 1754 onwards.[10] The guittar apparently became all the rage as a result of the actress Maria Macklin having played it in Samuel Foote's comedy *The Englishman in Paris* (première March 1753), and in a revival of John Fletcher's *The Chances* (première November 1754).[11] Giardini's engagement with the instrument at so early a date may have been a direct consequence of this sudden surge in its popularity.[12] Particularly fashionable with upper-class women, it often featured as a prop in society portraits, and it received the ultimate seal of approval in 1763 when Mortimer's *Director* announced that Hintz was 'Guitar-maker to Her Majesty and the Royal Family'. Such was the public's interest in the guittar that few musicians could afford to ignore it, and it quickly became part of their portfolio of teaching activities. Apart from Giardini, several string players – including the violinists Giovanni Battista Marella and Giovanni Battista Noferi, as well as the 'cellists James Oswald and Pasqualino di Marzi – composed for, and presumably taught, the instrument; Geminiani even wrote an instruction manual for it. Giardini's principal works for the guittar are: *VI Trii per cetra, violino e basso* (London, 1760), and *Six trios for the guittar, violin and pianoforte (or harp, violin and violoncello)*, Op. 18 (London, 1775).

Music purchases

The account of Giardini's numerous purchases of printed music at Cox's shop represents a new and significant source of information about the repertoire that English audiences heard during the early 1750s. We know that Giardini made his mark on public consciousness not only as a virtuoso but also as a performer and composer who embraced the latest continental trends. Indeed, Burney regarded his arrival on the London concert scene as something of a milestone in the evolution of the nation's musical taste:

> Handel's compositions for the organ and harpsichord, with those of Scarlatti and Alberti, were our chief practice and delight, for more than fifty years; while those of Corelli, Geminiani, Albinoni, Vivaldi,

---

10 *Public Advertiser* for that date.
11 Miss Machlin was taught by Thomas Call, who referred to her success in those plays when advertising for pupils; see *Public Advertiser* 8 April 1755, and Jürgen Kloss, *The 'guittar' in Britain 1753–1800*, 3–6, at the website: www.justanothertune.com/The GuittarinBritain1753-1800.pdf.
12 Other Schedule references to the guittar appear under the dates 29 May 1755 and 26 January 1756.

Tessarini, Veracini, and Tartini, till the arrival of Giardini, supplied all our wants on the violin, during a still longer period.[13]

If Giardini had the impact that Burney says he had, then it is important that we try to retrieve as much information as possible about the repertoire he fed to the British public. Some idea of prevailing musical tastes can of course be gleaned from the many concert advertisements included in contemporary newspapers; but, as we have seen, even where programmes survive, the amount of detail they give can vary enormously. The description of instrumental items in particular is often so brief and generic – 'Solo' or 'Concerto' followed by the name of the instrument and performer – as to be virtually useless for the purposes of identification. A consequence of this lack of detail has been the presumption among scholars that most players performed their own compositions at concerts.[14] Such a view, however, is surely too narrow an interpretation of what was in effect a default position, left deliberately ambiguous by performers and concert organizers alike in order to accommodate uncertainty over programming and last-minute changes of heart. Giardini, like other instrumentalists, undoubtedly did play his own music at many of the concerts in which he participated, but common sense dictates that he cannot have done so all the time. The range of publications that he bought from Cox supports this view, and suggests that his choice of repertory was less self-serving and more diverse than one might have expected from a composer/virtuoso keen to make an impression. Explicit data are neither easy to come by nor plentiful, but the number of occasions on which an advertisement expressly states that the performer will play one of his/her own compositions is more than matched by those in which the work specified is by someone else.[15] In a letter *From a Gentleman to a Lady, requesting her to accept his Tickets for a Concert* at the King's Arms in Cornhill, at which 'the new Master on the Violin, *De Giardini*', was to play, the sender writes:

> I shall be very happy if your Engagements permit you, Madam, to hear him at this Opportunity, for he has promised us a Solo by a very great

---

13 Charles Burney, *A general history of music from the earliest ages to the present period*. 4 vols. (London: for the author, 1776–89), 3:510. Burney later makes the point even more forcefully: '… we went on in tranquil enjoyment of the productions of Corelli, Geminiani, and Handel, at our national theatres, concerts, and public gardens, till the arrival of Giardini, Bach, and Abel; who … brought about a total revolution in our musical taste'; see *General history*, 4:673.
14 Catherine Harbor, 'The birth of the music business: public commercial concerts in London 1660–1750'. 2 vols. (Ph.D. dissertation, University of London, 2012), 1:167.
15 Three examples will suffice: at his London début in April 1751 Giardini included a Sammartini sonata in his programme; Chabran played a solo by Geminiani at his benefit on 26 March 1753; and later that year (17 May) Passerini performed a Tartini concerto at a subscription concert.

Master; and the great Misfortune of these Performers in general is, that they will play no Music but their own.[16]

Giardini, it would seem, was the exception to the rule. The purchases that Giardini made at Cox's shop on 30 November 1751 give no inkling of the reputation he later developed for advocacy of recent French and Italian music. Having only days before agreed to act as leader/soloist – and almost certainly artistic director – for Ogle's 1751–52 subscription series, he may have been looking for repertory by composers already familiar to English audiences; hence his acquisition of works by established names like Geminiani, Tartini and Robert Woodcock. The Geminiani entry must refer to his *Sonate a violino e basso ... Opera IV* (London: J. Walsh, 1739) for, according to the publisher's catalogue of *c.*1755, this was the only collection by the composer priced at £1 5s 0d.[17] The Woodcock publication, which is an old-fashioned set of concertos for woodwind instruments, is at first glance a curious choice for Giardini to have made. However, it is possible that he bought it for his collaborator in the Ogle series, the oboist and composer Thomas Vincent junior, who according to the newspapers performed an unspecified concerto in at least half of the twenty concerts in the series. It is unlikely that Vincent wrote these pieces himself, for as a composer he appears to have eschewed the concerto genre; that said, he may well have drawn on his own *Six solos for a hautboy[,] German flute, violin or harpsicord* [etc.] Opus 1 (London, 1748) on the half dozen or so occasions when he played a 'Solo' instead of a concerto.[18] Similarly, Giardini performed a solo at fifteen of Ogle's concerts, and it is possible that some of that repertoire was drawn from the Geminiani and Tartini prints supplied by Cox.

The value of new music as a commodity was unquestioned, however, and it is noticeable from Schedule A1 how often Giardini bought the latest musical publications near the beginning of a concert series; to quote Simon McVeigh: 'it was simply taken for granted that London subscription

---

16 'Letter CXII' in Charles Hallifax, *Familiar letters on various subjects* (London, 1754), 178–79. Giardini led the King's Arms Concert for the 1752 season, starting on Thursday 2 November; see *London Evening Post* 19–21 October 1752.
17 See 'A Catalogue of New Musick, and new Editions of Musick Printed for I. Walsh in Catharine Street in the Strand' [British Library call-mark: 7897.y.12. (3.)]. For further details, see William C. Smith and Charles Humphries, *A bibliography of the musical works published by the firm of John Walsh ... 1721–1766* (London: The Bibliographical Society, 1968), xiii (catalogue no. 25); and 159.
18 Vincent's *Solos*, originally printed by William Smith, were later issued under John Cox's imprint.

concerts would parade the most up-to-date music, often only just imported from the continent'.[19] Thus in January 1752, about a third of the way through the series with Ogle, Giardini acquired copies of Chabran's *Six sonates à violon seul et basse continüe* Opus 1, which had just arrived from Paris. Similarly on 26 January 1753, a few days into his series with Vincent, he bought Mondonville's *Pièces de clavecin en sonates avec accompagnement de violon ... Œuvre 3e*, which Walsh had published a week earlier as *Six sonates or lessons for the harpsicord which may be accompanied with a violin or German flute*. Giardini's purchases around this time mostly reflect his changed circumstances and the sort of music he considered appropriate to the subscription series he was organizing with Vincent. Solos such as the Mondonville would still have been required, of course; but with another high melody instrument at his disposal, Giardini's programming options expanded to include the vast repertoire of trio sonatas.[20] It therefore comes as no surprise to find that on 7 February he bought a large selection of works in that genre. His first purchase probably comprised single copies of three works by Giuseppe Sammartini: his *XII Sonate a due violini, e violoncello, e cembalo ... Opera Terza* (London: J. Walsh, 1747); the *XII Sonatas for two German flutes or violins with a thorough bass* (London: J. Walsh, c.1730); and *Six sonatas for two German flutes or two violins with a thorough bass for the harpsicord or violoncello ... Opera Sexta* (London: J. Walsh, 1750). Priced at 10s 6d, 5s 0d and 5s 0d respectively in the Cox and Walsh catalogues, the total cost of these prints would have been £1 0s 6d. Cox advertised two sets of Lampugnani sonatas for ten shillings under the heading 'Sonatas *or* Trios *for two* Violins *and a* Bass', and offered two sets of Besozzi's sonatas for sale also at ten shillings under 'Sonatas *or* Trios *for two* German-flutes *and a* Bass'. Walsh brought out Morigi's six trio sonatas in October 1751, priced at five shillings; this must be the collection to which the Schedule refers, for the composer's solo sonatas Opus 2 did not become available until John Johnson published them in 1757. Together, the Lampugnani, Besozzi and Morigi publications would have amounted to £1 5s 0d. The entry relating to Tessarini and Ciampi is too imprecise to yield much information, but the latter composer did of course write several trio sonatas,[21] and it is possible that the Tessarini collection was his *Six sonatas*

---

19 Simon McVeigh, 'Introduction', in *Concert life in eighteenth-century Britain*, ed. Susan Wollenberg and Simon McVeigh (Aldershot: Ashgate, 2004), 1–15, at 4.
20 Vincent was probably proficient on the flute and recorder as well as the oboe, as were many professional wind players in England at the time; see David Lasocki and Helen Neate, 'The life and works of Robert Woodcock, 1690–1728', *The American Recorder* 29/3 (August 1988), 92–104, footnote 79.
21 See Appendix 2: *s.v.* Ciampi, Vincenzo (?1719–62).

for two German flutes or violins with a thorough bass for the harpsicord ... *Opera Terza*, which Walsh issued in 1752 at five shillings.

The identity of the set of 'Martinis Concertos' that Giardini acquired on 19 January 1754 is similarly problematic. The half dozen E strings that he purchased at the same time would have come to three shillings, from which we can calculate the cost of the publication. According to the Walsh and Cox catalogues, the only collection of Sammartini concertos at nine shillings was the *Six concertos in 8 parts, for violins, french horns, hoboys, &c., with a bass for the violoncello and harpsichord. Compos'd by Sig.^{r} Gio: Bat: S^{r}Martini of Milan and Sig.^{r} Hasse* (London: J. Walsh, 1751). There are, however, other possibilities. On 17 January, a couple of days before Cox made this entry, Walsh published Giuseppe Sammartini's *Concertos for the harpsichord or organ with the instrumental parts for violins etc. Opera Nona.* The price was 10s 6d, so Giardini must have negotiated a good discount if this was the collection he bought. Also at 10s 6d were Sammartini's *VI Concerti grossi con due violini, alto-viola, e violoncello obligati; e due violini e basso di rinforzo* Op. 2 (London: J. Simpson, 1745), and his Concertos Op. 5 (1747) and Op. 8 (1752), both published by Walsh. Having just embarked on the subscription series with Chabran – their first concert was on 14 January 1754 – Giardini was perhaps looking out for new repertory for the forthcoming season. If that was his intention, then the idea of including Sammartini's music must have been quickly abandoned, for it does not feature in any of the programmes printed in the *Daily Advertiser* for that series.

During the late spring and summer of most years covered by Schedule A1 Giardini purchased from Cox large quantities of music, usually multiple copies of his own compositions at the discounted price of eight shillings. Thus he acquired '1 Dozen Sonatas' in May 1752, two copies of the same publication a year later, fourteen in May 1754 (twelve at £4 16s 0d plus two at 16s), and six more the following July. Very likely, these were to be re-sold to local music-shops and/or appreciative audience members at the venues at which he played while on tour – the eighteenth-century equivalent of the practice commonly deployed by visiting soloists and ensembles today who promote themselves by selling CDs of their performances from a merchandise display in the foyer of concert-halls. In May 1755 Giardini bought three more copies of his Sonatas, as well as Ferrari's *Six sonatas for a violin and a bass* (London: J. Cox, 1755) and Walsh's edition of Rameau's *Pièces de clavecin en concert*, which he probably used on tour. The six copies of each of his Sonatas, Solos, Songs and Violin Duets that he acquired in July 1756 may have been intended for re-sale on the Continent, where Giardini apparently spent part of that summer and autumn.

The entry recording Giardini's purchase of forty-nine books of unspecified songs on 10 March 1755 is intriguing. That was the date of his Dean

Street benefit, at which stars from the Opera, including Regina Mingotti and Rosa Curioni, had undertaken to perform.[22] The diva Mingotti in particular would have been a major attraction, and Giardini may have been thinking of ways to exploit her box-office appeal, while at the same time promoting more generally the interests of the opera house that employed them both. The vocal items on the concert programme probably included excerpts from the three operas already performed at the King's Theatre that season, namely *Ipermestra* (Hasse/Lampugnani), *Penelope* (Hasse/Galuppi) and *Siroe, Rè di Persia* (Lampugnani). 'Favourite Songs' from these works had already been extracted and published separately by John Walsh, and it is likely that the '49 Books of Songs' for which Cox billed Giardini on the day of his benefit consisted of a selection of those prints. Each set of songs retailed at two shillings and sixpence, but Giardini acquired them at the discounted price of two shillings, enabling him to make a small profit on every copy sold at the concert. However, as we now know, Mingotti was indisposed on the day, which must have been a great disappointment not only to the audience but also to Giardini, who was doubtless hopeful of making a financial killing from a full house.

Giardini was a great admirer – possibly even a lover – of Mingotti, and during the period they worked together he lent her moral support in the various battles she fought with the King's Theatre management.[23] He and most of the Opera's subscribers must have been amazed to discover that, of the six numbers that Walsh printed from *Siroe*, three were sung by Ricciarelli and only one by Mingotti. As a prima donna of international standing she would have been justified in taking this as a personal affront, for it put her on a par with the other, much less reputed, female members of the company – Curioni and Colomba Mattei – who were also represented by single songs in Walsh's collection. It must have been Giardini who, in an attempt to redress the balance, persuaded Cox to bring out *The two favourite songs in the opera call'd Siroe, sung by Sign^{ra} Mingotti*. This appeared on 15 March 1755 'by particular Desire', and contained 'D'ogni amator la fede' and 'Non vi piacque, ingiusti dei'.[24] Two days later, Cox debited a guinea

---

22 See page-one notices in the *Public Advertiser* and *Daily Advertiser* for Monday 10 March 1755.
23 See Michael Burden, *Regina Mingotti: Diva and impresario at the King's Theatre, London*. Royal Musical Association Monographs 22 (Farnham: Ashgate, 2013), 53.
24 See the *Public Advertiser* for that date. The attempts of Giardini and Mingotti to usurp Walsh's monopoly on publishing 'Favourite Songs' from the London stage are discussed in Burden, *Regina Mingotti*, 77–80. Burden's suggestion, however, that the arias Cox issued were 'Mingotti's own property' (78) is undermined by the attribution of at least one of them ('Non vi piacque') to Lampugnani in a concordant manuscript source; see *US-CA*: John Milton Ward, private collection (RISM ID no. 900010643).

from Giardini's account for 'binding a Book in Morocco and Gilt'. The special treatment lavished on this volume suggests that Giardini intended it as a gift, and one is tempted to conclude that it was a presentation copy for Mingotti of *The two favourite songs*, perhaps with Walsh's *Siroe* gobbets bound in with it.[25]

Other expenses

Incidental costs listed for 11 and 12 March 1755 almost certainly relate to Giardini's benefit on the tenth, discussed above: 'To 4 Gal*lon*^{s} of Rum £2 8s 0d'; 'To 2 Loaves of Sugar 15s 3½d'; 'To 1 Chauldron of Coals £1 16s 0d'; 'To ye Maid 10s 6d'.[26] Élite patrons attending a Dean Street concert on a chilly evening in early spring would certainly have expected the luxury of a warm room. Mr Ogle realized this back in 1751, as had concert promoters at other London venues before him.[27] However, it is clear that on this occasion Giardini went to more trouble than usual to ensure the comfort of both patrons and performers. The extra hospitality, in the form of a hot rum toddy, may have been his way of enhancing the experience of his aristocratic clientele. Similarly, the cauldron of coals appears to have been additional to the heating usually provided by the venue's management; this may have been laid on specially for Mingotti, Giardini being well aware that she was nursing the cold that had prevented her from singing at the Opera two days earlier.[28]

Advertising costs[29]

A number of entries clearly relate to Giardini's activity as both performer and concert-promoter. In this latter capacity he was ably assisted by Cox, who appears to have organized the publicity for his subscription series and benefits. Cox's responsibilities did not end there, however. Within nine

---

25 For a study of the 'Favourite Songs' phenomenon, see Michael Burden, 'From London's Opera House to the Salon? The *Favourite* (and not so "Favourite") *Songs* from the King's Theatre', in *Beyond boundaries: Rethinking musical circulation in early modern England*, ed. Linda Austern, Candace Bailey and Amanda Eubanks Winkler (Bloomington and Indianapolis: Indiana University Press, 2017), 223–37.
26 A 'London chaldron' of coals was 3156 lbs, that is, just under a ton and a half; see *Oxford English Dictionary, s.v.* 'chaldron'.
27 *General Advertiser*, 14 December 1751; Harbor, 'The birth of the music business', 1:202–03.
28 For Vanneschi's installation of stoves in the King's Theatre at this time, see Burden, *Regina Mingotti*, 33.
29 This section should be read in conjunction with Appendix 1.

Giardini's account at Cox's music shop 89

months of arriving in England, Giardini had apparently assumed the role of agent or sponsor of musicians visiting London from his native Savoy and other parts of north Italy, and Cox found himself having to manage the publicity for their concerts too. Mention has already been made of the initial support given to Chabran early in 1752, and other performers from north Italy – including the Colla brothers from Brescia and Federico Dellavalle, 'Bassoon to his Majesty the King of Sardinia' – followed shortly afterwards.[30] We learn from Schedule A1 that Cox produced five hundred tickets and two hundred large bills for the Collas toward the end of January 1752, almost certainly for their London début at the Little Theatre on 4 February. Giardini led the band for that concert, as he did for the Dellavalles' benefit later in the year.[31]

Between February and April 1752 Cox incurred a number of expenses preparing for a 'Concert of Vocal and Instrumental Musick' held at Dean Street on 10 April. This was Giardini's first benefit in London, an occasion for which he garnered an impressive array of musical talent – Frasi, Galli, Vincent, Pasqualino, Miller and the Colla brothers – in the hope of attracting a large audience of the best quality. The event had originally been planned for the day before, but for some reason it was re-scheduled and patrons were advised that 'Tickets delivered for the 9th will be taken the 10th'.[32] Cox began the task of marketing the concert on 11 February by ordering two hundred bills at a cost of six shillings, and a few days later he assembled the materials needed to engrave the admission-tickets. Although such items are by their very nature ephemeral, a number – particularly of the more decorative type designed and engraved for Giardini by Giovanni Battista Cipriani and Francesco Bartolozzi – survive from the 1760s onwards; tickets dating from the 1750s, on the other hand, are much rarer.[33] On 5 March Cox paid for an unspecified number of handbills, and eight days later he charged Giardini for running off eight hundred tickets, presumably for the same event. The Great Room, Dean Street,

---

30 For Chabran and the Collas, see Appendix 2. The King of Sardinia, Charles Emmanuel III (1701–73), was also Duke of Savoy. Dellavalle and his daughter took a benefit at the Little Theatre in April 1752, and he performed at the Concert Spirituel in Paris later that year; see Constant Pierre, *Histoire du concert spirituel 1725–1790* (Paris: Société française de Musicologie, 2000), 116 and 263, and James B. Kopp, *The bassoon* (New Haven, CT, and London: Yale University Press, 2012), 70. On 3 April 1752 Cox published the *Six sonatas Op. 5* by 'Sig. Alexandro Bezozzi, Musician in Ordinary to the King of Sardinia'; see *London Daily Advertiser* for that date.
31 *Daily Advertiser* 4 February 1752 and *General Advertiser* 17 April 1752.
32 *Daily Advertiser* 8–10 April 1752. A feature of Giardini's subsequent career is the freedom with which he changed the date of engagements.
33 But see Illustration 5.1 below.

had a gallery as well as a pit,[34] but its seating capacity cannot have been more than about five hundred; the figure of eight hundred may therefore represent a retrospective totting-up of the number of tickets printed both for the original and revised concert dates.[35] The entry for 16 March, 'To advertizeing your Benefit', refers to the seven-line notices placed in the *Daily Advertiser* on the 19th and 21st instant, which give the old date for the concert. London newspapers at the time offered to print advertisements 'of a moderate Length' for two shillings, but it is impossible to establish hard-and-fast rules about rates, as most printers apparently made individual decisions about each submission.[36] By the 1730s a standard ten- to twelve-line block cost between 1s 6d and 3s 6d, based on surviving printers' records, so three shillings was probably about right for a seven-line advert in 1752. The Schedule entry inserted between 18 March and 7 April almost certainly relates to publicity for the Dellavalle benefit on 17 April; at a cost of £1 4s (i.e. three shillings each), eight notices appeared in the *London Daily Advertiser* (2 April) and the *General Advertiser* (2, 3, 9, 14–17 April). The entries for 7 April – 'Hand Bills' (probably two hundred of them) and 'Advertizeings' (the *Daily Advertiser* 8–10 April) – publicized the new date of Giardini's benefit on the tenth.[37]

The Schedule entry for 27 February 1753 possibly concerns the Vestris benefit originally planned for Dean Street on 27 March, but which was aborted and re-scheduled to 12 April. As was the case with Giardini's 1752 benefit, the number of tickets produced (700) is probably the cumulative total for both dates, and the added expense of 'altering a Plate' rather supports this retrospective reading of the evidence. The entry dated 15 March is for advertisements in the *London Daily Advertiser* (16 March) and the *Daily Advertiser* (17, 20 and 22 March), which appear to have cost 4s 6d each. The five hundred bills ordered on 5 April must relate to the revised date of Vestris's benefit, but the entry for five hundred 'Card Ticketts' that immediately follows is most likely to have been for Giardini's Dean Street benefit early in May; this would be consistent with Cox's usual practice of organizing the tickets for an event about a month in advance (see Illustration 5.1). The entry for 26 April is more equivocal and requires a

---

34 *Public Advertiser* 15 March 1753; *London Chronicle* 1–4 March 1760.
35 On 1 May Cox debited Giardini's account for 'altering a Copper Plate'; if this was for changing the date on the plate from which the tickets were re-printed, then this is another example of a retrospective charge.
36 James Raven, *Publishing business in eighteenth-century England* (Woodbridge: Boydell Press, 2014), 129. Discounts were also available for regular clients and for adverts placed continuously over prescribed periods.
37 Eight shillings, instead of nine, was probably a concessionary price for the three consecutive advertisements.

Illustration 5.1 Red ticket for Giardini's benefit concert in May 1753. © The Trustees of the British Museum.

measure of conjecture to explain it. We know from press advertisements that Giardini's benefit was re-scheduled from 11 to 10 May, and to apprise the public of this change he may have asked Cox to produce five hundred handbills with the new date.[38] However, to avoid confrontation with the latter, who had already printed the tickets and was being inconvenienced yet again, he may have delegated to Vestris the task of placing the order, hoping at the same time that her charms might defuse the situation.[39]

Most revealing of all is Cox's meticulous account of the costs incurred during the Giardini/Chabran season, particularly with respect to the marketing techniques and practices that have come to light from correlating the Schedule entries with contemporary press advertisements and the concert-dates. Cox began promoting the series in the last weeks of 1753, placing notices with essential information – start-date, venue, number of concerts, performers, cost of tickets, and so on – in the *Daily Advertiser*

---

38 'Tickets delivered out for the 11th instant will be taken that Day'; see *Daily Advertiser* 2, 3, 9, 10 May 1753.
39 It is perhaps significant that Cox did not pay for the *Daily Advertiser* notices mentioned in footnote 38, Giardini having no doubt organized his own publicity in this instance.

on 17 December and the four days following.[40] Each advert now cost five shillings and he paid for them in advance, billing Giardini on 18 December for £1 5s. On the 28th instant Cox set in motion a second wave of publicity, with notices in the same newspaper for that and the following day, as well as 31 December to 3 January; at five shillings each, the cost of these advertisements came to £1 10s. On the day of the first concert (14 January 1754), he reinforced the information already disseminated with a leafleting campaign of 400 handbills. After this initial burst of activity advertising was allowed to tail off, and on 18 January he paid ten shillings for newspaper notices that appeared on the 19th and 21st instant, the latter date being that of the second concert in the series. Thereafter, Cox alerted patrons on the day of the concert only, that is on 28 January, 4, 11, 18, 25 February, and 4, 11 and 18 March, paying for the advertisements usually two days before the event.[41]

As soon as the subscription series was over, Cox turned his attention to organizing the benefit at Dean Street that Giardini and Vestris had planned for the following Monday (25 March). The printing of 600 tickets for this concert, at a cost of four shillings per hundred, had been in hand since 28 February, and he now focussed on more immediate publicity matters, spending £1 7s on 900 bills (i.e. three shillings per hundred) and, a day later, £1 5s on five advertisements in the *Daily Advertiser* (20–23 and 25 March).

Subsequent Schedule references to the cost of advertising concerts are more perfunctory and laconic. On 10 March 1755, for instance, Cox debited Giardini's account to the tune of £15 2s 0d for 'the Expences of you^r Benefitt', which had taken place at Dean Street that day. This summary charge must have encompassed newspaper notices, bills and perhaps the hire of the venue; there may also have been additional publicity costs, for Giardini had originally planned the event for the following Thursday (13 March), but subsequently brought it forward. Similarly with his 1758 benefit held at Dean Street on 13 February; there is only one item of expenditure on the Schedule relating to this event, namely for 'Advertizing' that is traceable in both the *Public Advertiser* and *Daily Advertiser* on 2, 3, 10, 11 and 13 February. Remarkably, the cost of these notices (£2 10s 0d) remained stable at five shillings each, despite the fact that advertising became more

---

40 Cox advertised only in the *Daily Advertiser* at this time, a fact that has completely masked the Giardini/Chabran series from users of the Burney newspaper collection, which has large lacunae in its holdings of that title.

41 On 23 February he paid nine shillings for advertising the concerts on 25 February and 4 March; this is probably an error for ten shillings, although it is conceivable that he obtained a discount.

expensive from the middle of 1757 when the government doubled the tax on every classified announcement from one shilling to two.[42]

The Schedule entries that most clearly define the services provided by Cox are dated 9 and 10 December 1755. These record the cost of press advertisements for 'The favourite Song[s] in the Opera called IL DEMOFOONTE, sung by Signora Mingotti', which could 'be had at Signor Degiardino's Lodgings, at the Royal Jelly-house in Pall-mall' and elsewhere.[43] Jommelli's *Demofoonte* received its first London performance at the King's Theatre on 9 December 1755 and ran for another nineteen nights – more than any other opera that season. Cox therefore lost no time in bringing the Mingotti songs to the public's attention; it is likely, however, that the costs of advertising them were entered in the wrong order on the Schedule. Newspaper evidence suggests that Cox paid nine shillings not on the 10th but on the 9th instant, that is, the day of the opera's première – probably for the notices that appeared next day in the *Public Advertiser* and *Daily Advertiser*. It then follows that the announcements placed on the 10th were for the 11th (*Public Advertiser*), 12th (*Public Advertiser* and *Daily Advertiser*) and the 16th (*Daily Advertiser*), and it was they that cost eighteen shillings. The fact that Giardini footed the bill for these adverts again tells us something about his relationship with Mingotti at the time. Confusingly marketed as if part of John Walsh's well-known series of operatic excerpts, 'The favourite Songs' were actually titled *Four songs in the opera call'd Il Demofonte* [sic] *sung by Sig.^{ra} Mingotti*. The collection as advertised claimed to have 'his Majesty's Royal Privilege', but this has not been verified and no patent was published with the music. Walsh for once, it seems, was upstaged and did not produce his own selection from the score until 23 December. As with *The favourite songs in ... Siroe*, his *Demofoonte* extracts accommodated Mingotti's music only once – and minimally at that – as part of a duet with Ricciarelli.[44]

---

42 Raven, *Publishing business*, 128.
43 *Daily Advertiser* and *Public Advertiser* 10 December 1755.
44 As managers of the King's Theatre during the 1756-57 season, Mingotti and Giardini were able to cut off Walsh's hitherto steady supply of operatic selections and publish their own. By 2 April *Favourite songs* 'sung by Sig.^{ra} Mingotti' in *Alessandro nell'Indie*, *Il re pastore* and *Antigono* had been 'Printed ... for the Proprietor' and were available from a list of music-sellers that did not include Walsh. Cox's name, too, is conspicuously absent – a sign, no doubt, of the widening rift that had developed between him and his business partner. Although each set of songs has its own title-page, pagination is continuous; that is: 1–[24], 25–40 and 41–58. Three of the four excerpts from *Alessandro* bear the ascription 'Del Sig: DeGiardini'.

Giardini's picture

Perhaps the most thought-provoking of the few entries that fall outside the categories discussed above is the ante-penultimate item on Schedule A1, which appears under the year 1758, on or after 10 February:

	£	s	d
To a Picture	6	6	0

Without more information, the subject of this work of art is likely to remain a matter of conjecture. All is not lost, however, for there are some very suggestive clues. The price of six guineas, which probably included the cost of the frame and carriage, means that the picture is likely to have been a head-and-shoulders portrait − perhaps of Giardini himself. Three images of the composer from around this time survive: a drawing attributed to Sir Joshua Reynolds dated to c.1755, now in the Ashmolean Museum, Oxford; an unfinished portrait by the same artist painted in 1760, at present in a private collection;[45] and a standard-sized canvas by Thomas Gainsborough, in the collection of Lord Sackville at Knole House, near Sevenoaks in Kent (Illustration 5.2). It is likely that the latter portrait is the one to which the brief entry on the Schedule refers. Gainsborough's genuine passion for music has been much written about by art historians and musicologists alike, as has the nature of his executant skills on a range of instruments; he had a passing acquaintance with the harp, harpsichord and viola da gamba, and according to the oboist and composer W. T. Parke he was 'an excellent violin player'.[46] He counted a number of musicians among his circle of friends, and several of his pictures depict musical themes; he was intimate with the Linley family, many of whom he painted, and his other sitters included Carl Friedrich Abel, Johann Christian Bach, Johann Christian Fischer and the formidable Ann Ford. Giardini and Gainsborough became boon companions and their close friendship is well documented in the latter's correspondence.

The Giardini canvas measures 30 × 25 inches (76.2 cm × 63.5 cm) and comes early in Gainsborough's canon, expert opinion unanimously assigning

---

45 David Mannings, *Sir Joshua Reynolds: A complete catalogue of his paintings*. 2 vols. (New Haven, CT, and London: Yale University Press, 2000), 1:217 and pl. 498. It is worth noting that a William Cox may have owned the Reynolds portrait; could he have been related to John?
46 William Thomas Parke, *Musical memoirs*. 2 vols. (London, 1830), 1:335.

Giardini's account at Cox's music shop 95

Illustration 5.2 Thomas Gainsborough, Portrait of Giardini (oil on canvas) *c.*1758. Knole House, Kent. Image: Witt Library, Courtauld Institute of Art, London, by courtesy of Lord Sackville.

it to the early 1760s.[47] In terms of portraiture it is classified as a 'head' or 'three-quarter', as it measured three quarters of a yard. From the little evidence we have for the artist's scale of prices at various points in his career, it is apparent that in 1758 five guineas was what one would have expected to pay for a head-and-shoulders by Gainsborough, a rate confirmed by his friend Philip Thicknesse.[48] The small number of Gainsborough's receipts that have survived tell us that in 1759–60 he raised his prices to eight

---

47 Ellis Waterhouse, *Gainsborough* (London: Edward Hulton, 1958), 70; Charles Cudworth, *Gainsborough, English music and the Fitzwilliam* (Cambridge: Fitzwilliam Museum, 1977), 12; Lindsay Stainton, *Gainsborough and his musical friends* (London: Greater London Council, 1977), no. 3 [no pagination]; *The letters of Thomas Gainsborough*, ed. John Hayes (New Haven, CT, and London: The Paul Mellon Centre for Studies in British Art, Yale University Press, 2001), 57.
48 *A sketch of the life and paintings of Thomas Gainsborough Esq.* (London, 1788), 17.

guineas for this the smallest standard size of portrait; see, for instance, those of William Lee (April 1759) and George Lucy (February 1760).[49] Another pointer to the valuation of the Giardini head is the fact that in 1778 the Duke of Dorset bought it for five guineas. To identify the portrait with the picture mentioned in the 1758 part of the Schedule would require only a slight broadening of the time-frame already proposed for its composition. That Giardini should own a Gainsborough is not inconceivable, for we know that at one time he had in his possession the landscape called 'Figures before a Cottage', which now hangs in the Fuji Art Museum, Tokyo;[50] but as this is an autograph version of his first 'Cottage door' picture and dates from 1773, we cannot identify it with the painting referred to in the Schedule.[51]

Gainsborough certainly knew Giardini in Ipswich before moving permanently to Bath in the autumn of 1759.[52] This is clear from Gainsborough's letter to David Garrick, dated 27 July 1768, which includes the following account of an amusing incident during a concert there:

> you must know Sir whilst I lived at Ipswich, there was a benefit Concert in which a new Song was to be introduced, and I being steward, went to the honest Cabinet-maker who was our Singer instead of a better, and asked him if he could sing at sight, for that I had a new song with all the parts written out, yes Sir said he I can – upon which I order'd M^r. Giardini of Ipswich to begin the symphony and gave my Signal for the Attention of the Company; but behold a dead silence followed the symphony instead of the song; upon which I jumped up to the fellow: D – n ye Why don't you sing? did not you tell me you could sing at sight? Yes, please your honor I did say I could sing at sight, but not first sight.[53]

Any attempt to pin down this particular occasion would be to enter the realms of speculation, for the local newspapers are not as informative about performers and repertoire as the London ones. That said, there were

---

49 Hayes, *The letters of Thomas Gainsborough*, 182–85 (123) and (127).
50 Gainsborough referred to this composition as 'Cottage & ragged Family'; see Hayes, *The letters of Thomas Gainsborough*, 123 (27).
51 John Hayes, *The landscape paintings of Thomas Gainsborough: A critical text and catalogue raisonné*. 2 vols. (London: Sotheby, 1982), 1:451–52, cat. no. 106.
52 Hugh Belsey, *Oxford dictionary of national biography*, s.v. 'Gainsborough, Thomas (1727–88)'.
53 Hayes, *The letters of Thomas Gainsborough*, 56–57 (34).

two benefit concerts in Ipswich in 1757 – 'Mrs. Lane's' on 2 June and 'Mr. Gibbs's' on 1September; and two in 1758 – 'Mr. Gibbs's' on 18 May and 'Mrs. Lane's' on 17 August.[54] The composer Joseph Gibbs was organist of St Mary-le-Tower, Ipswich, and a good friend of Gainsborough, who painted his portrait *c.*1756; they were both members of the local Musical Society, and his benefit is the sort of event that Giardini and the artist might well have supported.[55]

---

54 Dates of the Ipswich concerts for the year following appeared in the *Ipswich Journal* on 1 January and 31 December 1757. More detailed notices of individual concerts in the surrounding area can be found in the *Ipswich Chronicle*.

55 The most recent catalogue raisonné of Gainsborough's work has revised the dating of Giardini's portrait in light of the evidence adduced above; see Hugh Belsey, *Thomas Gainsborough: The portraits, fancy pictures and copies after Old Masters*. 2 vols. (New Haven, CT, and London: The Paul Mellon Centre for Studies in British Art, Yale University Press, 2019), 1:392–93, which reproduces a high-definition colour photograph of the painting.

Conclusion

As a source of information about the musical life of mid-eighteenth-century London, the litigation between Giardini and Cox must rank as one of the most significant discoveries of recent years. The Exchequer documentation in particular is as remarkable for the kaleidoscopic range of issues that it raises as it is unique for the detailed nature of its coverage. The pleadings provide new insights into aspects of Giardini's career already known to us, such as his role in the subscription series with Ogle, Vincent and Frasi, and his joint management of the Opera with Mingotti. They also reveal aspects of his activity about which we were hitherto unaware: for instance, his sponsorship of musicians from northern Italy, the concert series with Chabran, and the circumstances surrounding the genesis of the publication known today as the *Four overtures*, which have long been a mystery. Schedule A1 in particular sheds light on the nuts and bolts of the Cox/Giardini business relationship. As an 'outsider' newly arrived in London, Giardini may have had neither the time nor inclination to build the network of professional and social contacts on which freelance musicians typically depended; to mobilize his entrepreneurial skills as quickly and effectively as possible, he needed the help of someone like Cox, who had intimate knowledge of local musical institutions and practices. As part of the unusual business arrangement that subsequently developed between them, Cox provided Giardini with a number of services as banker/money lender and accountant; publisher and music seller; instrument dealer and repairer; administrative assistant (at concerts and operas); and publicity manager and ticket agent. Cox was, in effect, Giardini's guide through the unfamiliar and often treacherous labyrinth that was London's music industry. Although he charged for some of these services, for others he received no remuneration. These were not acts of generosity on Cox's part, however, for he was a hard-headed businessman and as much of an opportunist as Giardini. At an early stage he realized that a music-trader had much to gain from maintaining an association with someone who was not only the most fêted musician in England,

but who also had ready access to continental editions that could be pirated with impunity. Cox's assessment of the money-making potential of his pact with Giardini was doubtless correct; unfortunately, he did not reckon on the composer's prodigal ways, which left his account at Simpson's shop permanently and substantially in the red.[1] Their quarrel over the printing of the 'Six Overtures' proved to be a watershed moment in their relationship; from that point on, Giardini ceased to use Cox's services and either self-published or turned to Parisian or other London publishing houses.

Having delegated to Cox many of the tasks that a self-managing musician would have done for himself, Giardini was free to cultivate his career as a teacher, performer, composer and concert promoter. His modern virtuosity and dynamic leadership transformed musical standards in London during the 1750s, and under his influence concert life achieved a new prominence. While the intense period of concert activity that he inspired was short-lived – London had to wait until 1764 before a permanent concert structure was established – Giardini's series were the first to make concert-going central to the cultural life of the capital. As a virtuoso and the prime exponent of the new Italian *galant*, he was able to access the upper echelons of British society more easily than any other performer of the time. As a consequence, instrumentalists achieved a more elevated status: 'Concerts now counted for as much as the opera in the musical world; leading performers such as J. C. Bach and Felice Giardini became just as fashionable as Italian opera singers'.[2]

Burney admired Giardini for his business acumen and musicianship, and acknowledged 'the effects of his superiority on the violin in pursuing the progress of that instrument in this country';[3] but he was also well aware of his many character flaws, and it was on these that he chose to dwell towards the end of his entry on the composer in Rees's *Cyclopaedia*. One must, of course, read that vitriolic account of Giardini's temperament in the light of their unsuccessful joint ventures, which Burney believed had

---

1 Burney attests to Giardini's extravagance a number of times in the article on him in Abraham Rees, *The cyclopaedia, or, universal dictionary of arts, sciences, and literature*. 39 vols. (London: Longman, Hurst, Rees, Orme & Brown, 1819–20), 16 [no pagination]. When the Rev. Martin Madan, a good friend of the composer's, asked him why he was always short of money, he replied: 'I candidly confess, that I never in my life had five guineas in my pocket, but I had a *fever* till they were gone'; see [Anon.], 'Memoir of Felice Giardini', *The Harmonicon* 5 (1827), 215–17, at 217.
2 William Weber, *The rise of musical classics in eighteenth-century England: A study in canon, ritual, and ideology* (Oxford: Clarendon Press, 1992), 146.
3 Charles Burney, *A general history of music from the earliest ages to the present period*. 4 vols. (London: for the author, 1776–89), 4:460.

cost him dear.⁴ One suspects, however, that there is more than a grain of truth in the portrait he paints, for it resonates in many ways with aspects of Giardini's personality noted elsewhere in this study. The following brief extract from Burney is particularly apposite:

> ... with the brightest intellects, and the clearest head for business, his temper renders it so impossible for any enterprize to thrive under his direction, that the most favourable and auspicious beginnings constantly end in enmity and misfortune. He is as inveterate and powerful an enemy to the opera, oratorio, pantheon, and public and private concerts, when they are not under his direction, as any ex-minister usually is to the government; and yet, notwithstanding the attraction of his performances, abilities as a composer, and experience as a manager, so much are his tricks and tyranny held in abhorrence by patentees and proprietors, that they would shut their shops, rather than open them by his assistance.⁵

These are sentiments with which Cox would surely have agreed.

---

4 For more details, see Roger Lonsdale, *Dr. Charles Burney: A literary biography* (Oxford: Clarendon Press, 1965), 150–53 and 227–28; and *Memoirs of Dr. Charles Burney 1726–1769*, ed. Slava Klima, Garry Bowers, and Kerry S. Grant (Lincoln, NE, and London: University of Nebraska Press, 1988), 194–96.
5 Rees, *The cyclopaedia*, 16: *s.v.* Giardini, Felice.

Appendix 1: Schedule A1

The first Schedule to which the above written Answer referrs[.]
The Particulars of all the Moneys due from the said Complainant to this Defendant[.]

[Column 1]

1751				£	S	D
July	9th		To Cash lent him as P^{er} his Note of Hand	20	0	0
Sep^r	21st		To D*itt*^{o}	21	0	0
Oct^r	31st		To a Violin Bow and Case	5	5	0
Nov^r	2^d		To Cash lent him as P^{er} his Note of Hand	28	9	0
	4th		To Violin Strings	0	2	4
	8th		To D*itt*^{o}	0	16	2
	26th		To D*itt*^{o}	0	5	4
	30th		To 1 Giminiani's Solos[1]	1	5	0
			To 2 Tartini's Solos[2]	0	11	0
			To 1 Woodcocks Concertos[3]	0	14	0
Dec^r	3^d		To Cash lent him as P^{er} his Note of Hand	12	12	0
	20th		To a new Neck to a Violin and 2 Bridges[4]	1	2	0
	23^d		To Cash paid Customhouse Duty for his plates	4	0	0
1752						
Jan:	7th		To a New Belly to a Violin	1	5	0
	10th		To 3 Bundles of Ring Strings and 2 Rings Silver	1	16	0
	21st		To a New Finger Board to a Violin	0	5	0
	22^d		To a Double Harpsicord	42	0	0
			To Mending a Violin	0	1	0
	25th		To a New Neck and Finger Board to a Violin	1	1	0
	28th		To 2 Ream of Imperial Paper[5]	6	6	0
			To printing 200 Books blue Paper and Sticking[6]	5	5	0
			To 5 Schabrans Solos[7]	2	12	6
			To Mr Mahoon as P^{er} Order[8]	0	12	6

Appendix 1 103

		To D*itt*° for Cola and 500 Ticketts and 200 large Bills[9]	2	0	6
	29th	To a New Belly to a Violin	1	5	0
Feb:	11th	To a New Belly to a Violin and Strings[10]	1	9	8
		To 200 Bills	0	6	0
	14th	To 1 Bundle of Ring 1st	0	10	0[11]
		To Card Paper and Copper Plate and Ingraving	2	8	6
	21st	To 21 Rings of 1st and 2[d] Strings	0	10	6
		To Altering a Violin and New Finger Board	0	14	0
	25th	To Cash lent him as P[er] his Note of Hand	6	6	0
Mar:	5th	To Hand Bills	0	8	0
	12th	To Violin Strings	0	3	4
	13th	To Musick Books and printing 800 Ticketts *etc*	3	12	0
	16th	To advertizeing your Benefit	0	6	0
	18th	To 4 Quire of Royal Paper	0	16	0
		To advertizing	1	4	0
April	7th	To Hand Bills	0	6	0
		To Advertizeings	0	8	0
		To 2 Minuet Books[12]	0	2	0
	28th	To a Violin Bow and Case	6	6	0[13]
May	1st	To altering a Copper Plate	0	6	0
	7th	To 1 Dozen Sonatas and Violin Case[14]	7	12	6
Oct[r]	10th	To 2 Seconds for a Bass	0	3	0
1753					
Jan:	26th	To 2 Mondivilli's Lessons[15] and a Violin	5	2	0
Feb:	7th	To 3 S[t] Martinis Sonatas *etc*	1	0	6
		To Lumpugnani's[16] Buzzozi's[17] *and* Moridges[18] Sonatas	1	5	0
		To Tessirini's[19] Ciampis[20] *etc etc*	3	13	0
	27th	To 700 Ticketts and altering a Plate	1	9	0
March	15th	To Advertizeing	0	18	0
	21st	To a Letter	0	0	10
	24th	To 1 Tartini's Solos[21]	0	6	0
	29th	To 1 Length of Silver 4th and 2 Bridges[22]	0	0	11
April	5th	To 500 Hand Bills	0	18	0
		To 500 Card Ticketts *etc*	1	0	0
[*Column 2*]					
		To 2 Rings Silve[r] 4th	0	2	0
	16th	To printing 100 Books of Solos and Paper Sticking *etc*	5	15	6
	26th	To 500 Bills Signora Vestris as P[er] Order	0	18	0
		To 2 Rings Silver 4th	0	2	0
		To Cola as P[er] Order[23]	4	3	4
May	18th	To Cash lent him as P[er] his Note of Hand	15	14	0
	21st	To a new Neck for a Violin	1	1	0
	28th	To 2 Books of Sonatas	0	16	0
	29th	To a new Neck to a Violin	1	1	0
June	2[d]	To Cash lent him as P[er] his Note of Hand	21	0	0
		To a New Neck to a Violin	1	1	0
		To Porters as P[er] your Order	0	4	0

(*Continued*)

104 *Appendix 1*

(*Continued*)

	6th	To 2 Dozen *and* ½ Ring 1st	0	9	0[24]
		To 4 Rings Silver 4th	0	4	0
		To 4 D*itt*° 3d	0	2	0
	18th	To a new Neck to a Violin	1	1	0
July	2d	To Cash lent him as P*er* his Note of Hand	21	0	0
	7th	To Carriage of Proofs	0	3	6
Nov*r*	7th	To a Guittar	1	1	0
		To 2 Bundles of Ring 1st	0	18	0[25]
		To 2 Rings Silver 4th	0	2	0
		To the Use of a Harpsicord	1	1	0
		To a large Mahogany Desk	1	11	6
		To Porters	0	4	0
Dec*r*	6th	To a New Neck to a Violin	1	1	0
	10th	To Cash lent him as P*er* Note of his Hand	20	0	0
	18th	To Advertizing	1	5	0
	28th	To D*itt*°	1	10	0
1754					
Jan	2d	To a New Neck to a Violin	1	1	0
		To a Violincello [*sic*] and Bow	10	10	0
	14th	To 400 Bills	0	18	0
		To Cash paid M*r* Ellicot as P*er* y*our* Order[26]	29	8	0
	18th	To Advertizing	0	10	0
	19th	To 1 Martinis Concertos *and* 6 Rings of 1st Strings	0	12	0
	26th	To Advertizing	0	5	0
	30th	To 1 Set of Sonatas *and* binding 4 Books	1	8	0
Feb:	1st	To 6 Rings of 1st	0	3	0
	2d	To Advertizing	0	5	0
	9th	To D*itt*°	0	5	0
	16th	To Advertizing	0	5	0
	23d	To D*itt*°	0	9	0
		To 1 Dozen *and* ½ of Ring 1st	0	9	0
		To 1 Dozen 2d *and* 4 Dozen of 3d	1	10	0
	28th	To 600 Benefit Ticketts	1	4	0
Mar	9th	To Advertizing	0	5	0
	12th	To D*itt*°	1	0	0
	17th	To D*itt*°	0	5	0
	19th	To 900 Bills	1	7	0
	20th	To Advertizing	1	5	0
May	1st	To Porters *etc*	0	2	10
		To 12 Books of Sonatas	4	16	0
	24th	To 2 Books of Sonatas	0	16	0
	27th	To 300 Ticketts Frasi as P*er* Order[27]	0	9	0
	29th	To 300 D*itt*° black[28]	0	9	0
June	14th	To fitting a Bass Bridge and Exchanging a Violin	1	2	6
[*Column 3*]					
July	26th	To 6 Books of Sonatas	2	8	0
Nov*r*	10th	To a Letter	0	2	0
	20th	To 1 Book of Sonatas	0	8	0

1755					
Jan:	7th	To Cash as P[er] Note of Hand	31	2	0
Feb:	26th	To 1 Book of Sonatas	0	8	0
		To binding 4 Books	0	8	0[29]
Mar:	7th	To a Porter	0	1	0
	10th	To 49 Books of Songs	4	18	0
		To Porteridge	0	2	0
		To the Expences of y*ou*r Benefitt	15	2	0
	11th	To 4 Gal*lon*s of Rum	2	8	0
		To 2 Loaves of Sugar	0	15	3½
		To a Porter	0	4	0
	12th	To 1 Chauldron of Coals	1	16	0
		To ye Maid	0	10	6
	17th	To binding a Book in Morocco and Gilt	1	1	0
		To 3 Books of Songs	0	6	0
April	14th	To Mr Winch[30]	10	9	6
May	1st	To a Porter	0	1	0
	3d	To binding 4 Books of Songs	0	8	0
		To 2 Books of Sonatas	0	16	0
	17th	To a Porter	0	1	0
	19th	To 2 Books of Farari's Solos[31]	0	10	0
		To binding 3 Books	0	6	0
		To a Porter	0	1	0
	23d	To 1 Book of Sonatas	0	8	0
	29th	To 1 Ramoso's Concertos[32]	0	10	6
		To binding 5 Books	0	10	0
		To a Guittar	2	2	0
June	13th	To 1 Giminianis Solos[33]	1	5	0
July	9th	To 36 Books Sent abroad	9	18	0
Augst	14th	To Carriage of Proofs	0	5	0
Sepr	16th	To D*itt*o	0	5	0
Decr	4th	To a Coach for Mr Penvold[34]	0	4	0
	9th	To Advertizing Signora Mingotti's Songs	0	18	0
	10th	To D*itt*o	0	9	0
1756					
Jan	5th	To a Manderlean	2	2	0
	26th	To 1 Bundle of Guitar Strings	0	8	0
		To 1 D*itt*o blue knot 1st	0	5	0
Mar:	30th	To 100 Books of Overtures	105	0	0
July	7th	To 6 Books of Songs	2	8	0
		To 6 D*itt*o Solos	2	8	0
		To 6 D*itt*o Sonatas	2	8	0
		To 6 D*itt*o Duetts	2	8	0
1757					
Sepr	23d	To 3 Bundles of Strings[35]	2	5	0
		To 1 Book of Overtures	0	18	0
Novr	26th	To 1 Book of Solos, 1 Book of Duetts, 1 Book of Sonatas and 1 Book of Songs	1	12	0
		To my Attendance at the Opera	30	0	0

(*Continued*)

106 *Appendix 1*

(*Continued*)

1758
Feb:	10th	To Advertizing your Benefit[36]	2	10	0
		To a Picture	6	6	0
		To my Attendance at Sundry times at your Subscription Concerts	42	0	0
		To Mrs Ogle[37] as Per Receipt	6	16	6[38]
			£670	3	8

[1] In the Cox catalogue of *c*.1753 (British Library call-mark: Hirsch III.225) the collection appears as '12 Solos, Op. 4a.' under the heading 'Solos *for a* Violin *and* Harpsicord', and cost £1 5s 0d. It should therefore not be confused with Geminiani's *XII Solo's for a violin with a thorough bass* – Walsh and Hare's edition of his *Sonate a violino, violone, e cembalo* [Opus 1] – which cost six shillings.

[2] Walsh published English editions of Giuseppe Tartini's *XII Solos for a violin with a thorough bass for the harpsicord or violoncello* (1742) and *Six solos for a violin … opera secunda* (1746). The list-prices in Cox's catalogue (*c*.1753) are six shillings and four shillings respectively; the entry may refer to the *XII Solos*, with a discount of one shilling given for buying two copies.

[3] Walsh first published Woodcock's *XII Concertos in eight parts* in 1727. In the Walsh catalogue (*c*.1755), the collection is priced at twelve shillings; for more information on the composer and his music, see David Lasocki and Helen Neate, 'The Life and Works of Robert Woodcock, 1690–1728', *The American Recorder* 29/3 (August 1988), 92–104.

[4] A new neck (and fingerboard) was a guinea (see 25 January 1752 below); the bridges must therefore have been sixpence each.

[5] This and the following reference possibly relate to Cox's re-printing of Giardini's *Duetti* Opus 2.

[6] Probably an error for 'Stitching'; see also entry for 16 April 1753.

[7] Chabran's *Six sonates à violon seul et basse continüe … 1er. oeuvre* (Paris, 1751) therefore cost 10s 6d; see Appendix 2.

[8] Presumably this is Joseph Mahoon, 'harpsichord maker to His Majesty', who worked in 'Marybone'(i.e. Marylebone) and Golden Square, London; for more information, see *New Grove Dictionary of music and musicians* (henceforth *NGD*). 29 vols. (2nd edn, London: Macmillan, 2001), 15:633–34. Evidently a man of wide interests and tastes, he subscribed to several publications in a range of disciplines, including Barnabas Gunn's *Two cantatas and six songs* (Gloucester, 1736), Henry Carey's *The musical century* (London, 1740), James Miller's *Miscellaneous works in verse and prose* (London, 1741), John Travers's *Eighteen canzonets for two and three voices* (London, 1745?), James Foster's *Discourses on all the principal branches of natural religion and social virtue* (London, 1749–50), Richard Langdon's *Ten songs and a cantata* (London, 1759), and John Rowe's revision of William West's *Mathematics* (London, 1762). Cox's payment of 12s 6d to Mahoon may have been for services relating to Giardini's purchase of a harpsichord six days earlier.

[9] See Appendix 2, *s. v.* Colla (Cola) brothers (*fl. c*.1740–*c*.1770).

[10] £1 5s 0d for a new belly and two sets of strings @ 2s 4d.

[11] Of the violin's strings, the E was the most likely to break and was therefore bought in large quantities. A 'bundle' probably consisted of thirty strings; see Alberto Bachmann, *An encyclopedia of the violin* (New York: D. Appleton & Co., 1925), 148.

[12] Possibly *A collection of [choice] minuets as they are performed at both theatres, and other publick assemblies, for the violin, German flute, and [or] hautboy, with a thorough bass for the harpsichord* (London: J. Oswald, 1752). Priced at one shilling, this collection was advertised on 2 April; see the *Daily Advertiser* for that date, and the *General Advertiser* for 7th and 20th instant.

Appendix 1   107

[13] If a violin case was £2 16s 6d (see footnote 14 below), then the bow cost £3 9s 6d; for a similar entry, see under 31 October 1751.

[14] A dozen copies of Giardini's sonatas would have cost him £4 16s (12 × eight shillings), so the case was priced at £2 16s 6d.

[15] The Cox catalogue prices the Walsh edition of Mondonville's Op. 3 at 10s 6d, so the violin cost £4 1s.

[16] Giovanni Battista Lampugnani (1708–88) came to London in 1743 to take up the post of composer in residence at the King's Theatre, which he held for a couple of seasons.

[17] The oboist and composer Alessandro Besozzi/Bezozzi (1702–93) was part of a large family of musicians active in Milan and the surrounding area. From the early 1730s till death he served the King of Sardinia, Carlo Emanuele III, as *virtuoso d'oboe* in the court chapel at Turin. On 25 March 1757, two unidentified members of the Besozzi family played an oboe concerto during a concert at Drury Lane that also featured the Hasse/Giardini oratorio *I pellegrini*. They also had a benefit at the Great Room, Dean Street, which took place on the following 28 April after several postponements. The *Six sonatas* that Cox published in 1752 as Alessandro's Opus 5 is a composite volume consisting of works selected from the composer's previous printed collections.

[18] Angelo Morigi, an Italian violinist and composer from Rimini, was active in London earlier than the date suggested by *NGD*, 17:119, *viz.* May 1751. He appeared at Hickford's Room on 23 April 1750, and was due to play there on the following 21 March, but the death of Frederick, Prince of Wales, the day before caused the concert to be postponed to 3 May; he also performed *gratis* at a benefit concert for Cuzzoni on the 23rd of that month. Walsh brought out Morigi's trios in 1751, the year in which he appears to have left London; nonetheless, his solos Opus 2 and concertos Opus 3 were published by John Johnson in 1757 and 1756 respectively. It is not clear when the composer returned to Italy, but he was in the service of the Duke of Parma *c.*1758.

[19] The Italian violinist and composer Carlo Tessarini (*c.*1690–*c.*1766) arrived in London in 1747, and was engaged as leader of the orchestra at Ruckholt House pleasure gardens in Essex, about four miles north-east of London. According to the *General Advertiser* for 18 May of that year, he introduced his audiences to 'some Curious Pieces of New Musick brought from Italy'. On 27 April 1748 he used the press to inform his subscribers that he was going abroad in four or five days, and by 1750 he was back in Italy.

[20] See Appendix 2, *s.v.* Ciampi (Chiampi), Vincenzo (?1719–62).

[21] See footnote 2 above.

[22] If a bridge was sixpence (see footnote 4 above), then this entry does not make sense.

[23] Advertisements for Signor Colla's benefit at the Little Theatre on 5 May 1753 show that tickets were available from a number of outlets, including Cox's music shop and Giardini's lodgings at the China Shop in Old Bond Street. The sum of £4 3s 4d may have been the ticket money that Giardini owed Colla, but which Cox paid for him.

[24] It is evident from elsewhere in the Schedule that a violin E string cost 6d; see, for instance, the entries under 1 and 23 February 1754. The quantity specified here must therefore be an error for '1 Dozen *and* ½ Ring 1st'.

[25] A 'bundle' of E strings cost ten shillings (see entry dated 14 February 1752), so Giardini must have received a discount for purchasing two.

[26] See Chapter 2, pp. 26–27. The Ellicotts were a well-known family of clockmakers in Sweeting's Alley, and Giardini may have bought a timepiece from them at some stage.

[27] This entry and the next most probably refer retrospectively to Frasi's benefit performance of Handel's *L'Allegro, il Penseroso ed il Moderato* at the King's Theatre on 25 April 1754, in which Giardini participated. According to the papers, tickets were 'to be had of Signora Frasi, at her House in Gerrard-street, Soho. Boxes may be had at Signora Frasi's, or at the Theatre'. She sang *L'Allegro* again in Oxford at the beginning of July, and possibly at Covent Garden on 23 May, but there is no reason why Cox would have prepared tickets for those occasions.

[28] The different types of ticket were sometimes distinguished by colour, though the coding was not always consistently applied. At the Giardini/Vincent subscription concerts the

108 Appendix 1

subscribers' tickets (presumably printed in black) admitted either a gentleman or a lady, but the red tickets admitted ladies only; see *Public Advertiser* 27 February and 5 March 1753. According to the terms for subscribers to the Bach/Abel concerts, 'The Ladies tickets are black, and the Gentlemens' red'; see *Gazetteer and New Daily Advertiser* for 12 January 1770.

[29] Two shillings appears to have been Cox's standard charge for binding folio-size music; see the entries under 3, 19 and 29 May 1755.

[30] See Appendix 2, *s.v.* Winch, Christopher (*fl. c.*1725–61).

[31] The Italian violinist and composer Domenico Ferrari (1722–80) was considered one of Tartini's best pupils. His Opus 1 set of *Six sonatas for a violin and a bass* (London: J. Cox, 1755) is undoubtedly the collection to which the schedule refers; the British Library's online catalogue is clearly mistaken in dating it speculatively to 1759, for on 15 March 1755 the *Public Advertiser* described it as 'just published'. Subsequent advertisements give the price as 5s, which serves as a further means of identification. Ferrari's output also includes *Six sonatas or trios for two violins or German flutes* (London: John Lavo, 1757), most of which are by Campioni; and *Six sonatas or duets for two violins* Opus 2 (London: J. Walsh, 1762), which he shared with Pietro Nardini.

[32] Jean Philippe Rameau's *Pièces de clavecin en concerts* (Paris, 1741) were issued by Walsh in 1750 as *Five concertos for the harpsicord ... accompanied with a violin or German flute or two violins or viola, with some select pieces for the harpsicord alone*. The price agrees with that in the Cox and Walsh catalogues.

[33] See footnote 1.

[34] Possibly James Penvold, attorney of Garlick Hill, Thames Street; see *Kent's directory* (London, 1760), 88, and Mortimer's *Universal Director* (London, 1763), 89.

[35] At fifteen shillings a bundle, these strings were possibly for a 'cello.

[36] Giardini's Dean Street benefit was on 13 February 1758; see *Public Advertiser* for that date.

[37] See Appendix 2, *s.v.* Mrs Ogle (*c.*1710–*c.*1765).

[38] According to Simon McVeigh, the Great Room, Dean Street, cost 5 guineas a night to hire in 1754; see *Concert life in London from Mozart to Haydn* (Cambridge: Cambridge University Press, 1993), 170. It is possible that by 1758 the price had risen to six and a half guineas (£6 16s 6d); having paid Mrs Ogle on Giardini's behalf, Cox took a receipt to reclaim his money.

Appendix 2: Giardini's associates

Chabran (Schabran), Charles (1723–54)

A member of a well-known Piedmontese family of musicians, Carlo Giuseppe Valentino Chiabrano learned the violin with his uncle, the composer and violinist Giovanni Battista Somis, who could count among his pupils some of the finest players in Europe (including Giardini). Chiabrano spent his formative years in Turin where, at the age of fourteen, he was engaged in the Sardinian royal chapel at an initial salary of 200 lire per annum; he also played alongside his father Giovanni Nicola in the orchestra of the Teatro Regio, remaining in post until at least 1743.[1] His movements thereafter are obscure until the period April–June 1751, when he appeared under the name of 'Chiabran' at the Concert Spirituel in Paris, where he received mixed reviews for his performances.[2] According to Fétis, Chabran taught the French violinist and composer Pierre Vachon around this time. His *Six sonates à violon seul et basse continüe ... 1er oeuvre* were published under the name of 'Mr Ghabran' in Paris in November 1751, and shortly afterwards he and his wife, who was a singer, moved to England. He made his London début at Ranelagh House on 18 January following, and three days later the couple gave a benefit concert of vocal and instrumental music at the New Theatre in the Haymarket, where they were supported by Frasi, Vincent and Pasqualino. Tickets for this event were available not only from Chabran's lodgings in St Martin's Street, but also from Giardini's in Covent Garden and from John Cox at Simpson's music shop. He was the first of many musicians from northern Italy whom Giardini promoted in London;

---

[1] Marie-Thérèse Bouquet-Boyer, 'Note biografiche sulla famiglia Chiabrano' in *Gaetano Chiabrano: 44 Sonate da camera*. Monumenti musicali italiani, xii: Monumenti di musica piemontese, 5. Libro 1: Sonate 1–15, ed. Aldo Pais (Milan: Suvini Zerboni, 1988), xv.

[2] See *Mercure de France*, May 1751, 187–88; and Charles Collé, *Journal historique, ou mémoires critiques et littéraires* (Paris, 1805), 379.

the latter's purchase from Cox of five copies of Chabran's sonatas on 28 January 1752 may testify to an early enthusiasm for his younger contemporary's work, but their mutual regard soon developed into a rivalry that the press was not slow to exploit. Signora 'Ciabran' sang in Frasi's benefit on 10 March following, sharing the platform with Giardini, Signor Colla and others, and two days later Charles played for Elisabetta Gambarini at the Great Room, Dean Street. On the 17th instant he and Giardini performed a solo in the first and second halves respectively of Miss Sheward's benefit, during which the first signs of tension between the two men surfaced.[3] In May the Chabrans were in Bath, where they gave a concert by command of the Countess of Cumberland for the benefit of Signora Chabran, 'lately come from Italy'.[4] The programme included an overture and a harpsichord concerto by her husband, which have since been lost. Over the next couple of years Chabran took part in numerous London concerts, including in 1753 Mr Philidor's Concert (23 February), the benefit for Decay'd Musicians (30 April), and the King's Arms Concert (15 November) which he led. Any differences he may have had with Giardini were put aside by January 1754, when they collaborated in a series of subscription concerts at Dean Street. A satirical pamphlet, *A scheme for having an Italian opera in London* (1753), bears witness to this reconciliation:

> 'Tis true that *Giardini* and *Chabran* have not been well together for some Months. A Thing quite natural. *Cæsar* was never a Friend to *Pompey*, *Augustus* to *Marc-Antony*; and these two Fiddle-Warriors very properly follow these great Examples. Yet, Thanks to *Apollo*, they are of late agreed to share the musical Glory between them; and it is to be hoped they will be true to one another, and prove for the future rather a *Marlborough* and a Prince *Eugene*.[5]

---

3 See the Inspector's column in the *London Daily Advertiser* for 23 March.
4 *Bath Journal* 11 May 1752.
5 Although anonymous, *A scheme* is undoubtedly the work of Giuseppe Baretti (1719–89), who was active in London as a translator, essayist and critic; he followed this attack on Vanneschi and his alleged mismanagement of the Opera with *The voice of discord, or the battle of the fiddles* (1753). I am grateful to Professor Michael Talbot for drawing my attention to the first of these publications; see also Jasmin Cameron and Michael Talbot, 'A many-sided musician: the life of Francesco Barsanti (c.1690–1775) revisited', *Recercare* xxv/1–2 (2013), 95–154, particularly 137-38. During the War of the Spanish Succession Prince Eugene of Savoy, one of the greatest soldiers of his generation, fought alongside the first Duke of Marlborough at the battle of Blenheim (1704) and in other theatres of conflict.

Chabran and Giardini also took part in Mrs Ogle's benefit on 4 April 1754, along with their wives. Less than six months after this event Chabran was dead and buried; he was laid to rest in St Pancras churchyard on 6 September 1754, the incumbent qualifying the entry in the parish register with the epitaph 'a famous performer on ye Violin'.[6] St Pancras cemetery served not only as a burial ground for its parishioners, but also for several foreign dignitaries and aristocrats, and it was the last resting place of many Roman Catholics from all around London. Chabran is therefore no more likely to have dwelled in the parish than is J. C. Bach, who was also buried there nearly thirty years later. Chabran's sonatas were not published in England until Peter Welcker brought out his edition in May 1763. Four days later Walsh included four of the set in his *Six favourite solos for a violin with a bass for the violoncello and harpsichord*, the other pieces in the collection being by Carlo Antonio Campioni.[7] The English and French editions differ very little, though the latter does include an additional composition entitled 'La Caccia'.[8]

Ciampi (Chiampi), Vincenzo (?1719–62)

Ciampi came to London in 1749 as successor to Natale Resta, composer and music director of the Italian *buffo* company, managed by Giovanni Francesco Crosa, which had been in residence at the King's Theatre since November of the previous year.[9] The troupe dispersed soon after Crosa was declared bankrupt in April 1750, but whereas most of its members returned to the Continent, Ciampi appears to have remained in London and earned a living teaching music privately. Among his later pupils was Lady Caroline Russell, only daughter of the fourth Duke of Bedford, to whom he taught

---

6 London Metropolitan Archives: P90/PAN1/005 (births, marriages and burials 1753–73); see also *Public Advertiser* for 10 September 1754.
7 *Public Advertiser* 27 May 1763.
8 A re-issue of the Parisian edition was advertised in the *Mercure de France*, May 1760, 177.
9 Some authorities believe that Ciampi was maestro from the beginning of Crosa's tenure at the King's; see François-Joseph Fétis, *Biographie universelle des musiciens et bibliographie générale de la musique*. 8 vols. (2nd edn, Bruxelles, 1860–65), 2:299; Richard G. King and Saskia Willaert, 'Giovanni Francesco Crosa and the first Italian comic operas in London, Brussels and Amsterdam, 1748–50', *Journal of the Royal Musical Association* 118/2 (1993), 246–75; *New Grove Dictionary of music and musicians* (henceforth *NGD*). 29 vols. (2nd edn, London: Macmillan, 2001), 5:830–32; and Patricia Howard, *The modern castrato: Gaetano Guadagni and the coming of a new operatic age* (Oxford: Oxford University Press, 2014), 28. However, the contract between Crosa and the earl of Middlesex, who invited the company to London in 1748, names Resta as its music director; see The National Archives of Great Britain (henceforth TNA): E 112/1216/2685.

112 *Appendix 2*

the harpsichord and singing.[10] On 27 April 1750, the day before the Crosa company's last performance, he was listed among the vocalists in Signora Giacomazzi's benefit concert at Hickford's Room, where he sang 'a Song of his Composition'.[11] He was certainly in London on 2 May 1753 when, according to the press, he played an unspecified role in a benefit for the castrato Nicola Ranieri at the Great Room, Dean Street. Ciampi's *Didone* was performed at the King's Theatre during the 1753–54 season, and his *La famiglia de' Bertholdi* was heard at Covent Garden in 1754–55, though the extent of his involvement in these productions is unclear. The double-bass player Stefano Storace, father of Nancy and Stephen junior, sued Ciampi in King's Bench in 1754, but further details have not survived.[12] Ciampi apparently led the ensemble that played for Miss Davies's benefit at Dean Street on 18 March 1755. He may have returned to Italy shortly before the following advertisement appeared in the London papers:

> The Creditors of Mr. Vincenzo Ciampi, late of Greek-street, Soho, next Door to the Turk's Head Tavern, are desired to bring in their Demands of what kind soever to Mr. Bottarelli, at the Blue Ball in Church-street, St. Ann's, who will attend to this Affair till Monday Se'nnight, from Nine in the Morning till Seven in the Afternoon'.[13]

The person charged with settling the composer's affairs was presumably Giovanni Gualberto Bottarelli, the poet who was later employed as librettist at the King's Theatre in the 1760s and 70s.[14] All of Ciampi's instrumental works were published in London. In April 1751 John Johnson brought out his *Six sonatas for two violins and a bass*, and another set of six appeared from the same press as 'Opera the Second' a month later, both priced at five shillings. At about the same time, Walsh produced two different sets of Ciampi trio sonatas, making publicly available twenty-four pieces in all. Johnson advertised the composer's 'Six new Overtures for Violins, French Horns, etc.' in the *Daily Advertiser* on 9 January 1754.

---

10 See Gladys Scott Thompson, *The Russells in Bloomsbury 1669–1771* (London: Jonathan Cape, 1940), 204–5.
11 *Daily Advertiser* 23 and 27 April 1750.
12 TNA: KB 125/153.
13 *Public Advertiser* 25 June 1755. Ciampi must have been a neighbour of Christopher Winch (see Appendix entry below), who ran the Turk's Head tavern during the 1750s.
14 See *NGD*, 4:83. A number of composers (Thomas Augustine Arne, John Worgan, Willem de Fesch, William Boyce, Claudius Heron and Samuel Howard) set twelve of his Italian translations of Horace's odes, some more than once; see *Del canzoniere d'Orazio di G. G. Bottarelli Ode xii, messe in Musica da' più rinomati Professori Inglesi* (London, 1757). Bottarelli was the librettist of Giardini's opera seria *Enea e Lavinia* (1764).

Colla (Cola) brothers (*fl. c.*1740–*c.*1770)

During the middle years of the eighteenth century the brothers Domenico and Giuseppe Colla, from Brescia in northern Italy, toured the principal cities of Europe demonstrating their mastery of 'two entirely new instruments', namely the *colascione*, and a smaller version of the same, the *colascioncino* or *colasciontino*.[15] Derived from the Middle Eastern 'long lute' or *tanbūr*, the *colascione* had a small lute-shaped body and a long narrow neck fitted with frets; typically it carried two or three strings which were played with a plectrum. A favourite instrument with *commedia dell'arte* performers and Neapolitan street singers, it occasionally found its way into contemporary *opera buffa*.[16] The brothers made their London début at a benefit on 4 February 1752, with Giardini leading, Giulia Frasi taking the vocal part, and Signor Colla performing 'a Solo on a new Instrument, called Calascioncino'.[17] Cox's payment of £2 0s 6d 'for Cola and 500 Ticketts and 200 large Bills' on 28 January must refer to this concert, which was held at the Little Theatre in the Haymarket, where an audience of about six hundred could be seated with relative ease.[18] On 24 February one of the Collas (probably Domenico) appeared at Hickford's Room in Signor Cattanei's benefit, again with Giardini but this time supported by the mezzo-soprano Caterina Galli; and on the last day of the month he joined Frasi and John Beard in a concert at Ranelagh House. After playing for Frasi's benefit on 10 March, Colla and Giardini took part in the benefit organized for the bassoonist Signor Dellavalle and his daughter, who sang some Italian songs.[19] The Little Haymarket was again the venue for Colla's concert on his return visit to London a year later, when Chabran took on the responsibility of first violin, the singers were Frasi and Signora Vestris, and Giardini played the harpsichord.[20] After that brief sojourn the brothers did not return to London for some thirteen years, during which time they performed 'in all the foreign Courts in Europe, where they met with great Encouragement and Applause; their Instruments being very extraordinary, and

---

15 Another pair of Italian brothers – Giacomo and Giuseppe Bernardo Merchi – who toured a lot but used Paris as their base, also popularized the instruments; see Daniel Fryklund, 'Colascione och colascionister', *Svensk Tidskrift för Musikforskning* 18 (1936), 88–118, James Tyler and Paul Sparks, *The early mandolin* (Oxford: Clarendon Press, 1989),138–39, and *NGD* 16:449–50, *s.v.* Merchi, Joseph Bernard.
16 See Michael F. Robinson, *Naples and Neapolitan opera* (Oxford: Clarendon Press, 1972), 221; and David Kimbell, *Italian opera* (Cambridge: Cambridge University Press, 1991), 318.
17 *Daily Advertiser* for that date.
18 Judith Milhous and Robert D. Hume, 'J. F. Lampe and English Opera at the Little Haymarket in 1732–3', *Music & Letters* 78/4 (November 1997), 502–31, at 509.
19 *General Advertiser* 17 April.
20 *Public Advertiser* 5 May 1753; this was Giardini's only known public performance on this instrument.

their Execution surprising'.[21] Pier Leone Ghezzi's caricature of the 'Brescians Domenico and his brother' (c.1752), showing them playing the *calasciontino* and guitar respectively, is undoubtedly a depiction of the Collas. A later printing of Matthias Oesterreich's copper-plate engraving of the drawing bears a subscription stating that they performed for Frederick the Great at Sanssouci Palace in April 1765 (Illustration App. 2.1). A manuscript in the Sächsische Landesbibliothek, Dresden, containing six sonatas for *colasciontino* by Domenico Colla, may be regarded as further evidence of the brothers' activity at the Prussian and Saxon courts.[22]

Mrs Ogle (c.1710–c.1765)

Mrs Ogle (née Mary Medcalf) operated the London concert venue known as the Great Room in Dean Street, Soho, for about a decade starting in late 1751, initially with her husband and then on her own. She married Cuthbert Ogle (b. 1706) at Horton by Blyth, Northumberland, on 17 July 1729 and had some ten children, all of whom were baptized in the then parish church of St Nicholas, Newcastle upon Tyne. Ogle's father, also called Cuthbert, was a yeoman farmer of Stickley. In the early 1730s, when he became heavily indebted, his creditors agreed to the transfer of his assets to his son in the hope that they would be better managed, but eventually both men were sued in Chancery for their debts.[23] In 1740 Cuthbert junior, 'confectioner', appeared at the Newcastle assizes accused of illegally exercising the trade of grocer, though he was later permitted to do so.[24] However, it was not long before he too was in financial straits, and by 1751 he and his wife had moved to London, where in March of that year 'Cuthbert Ogle, late of Newcastle upon Tyne, Merchant' appeared on a list of bankrupts.[25] Nothing daunted, Ogle instituted a series of weekly subscription concerts in Dean Street for the 1751–52 season, modelled perhaps on those that Charles Avison, organist of St Nicholas's, had established in Newcastle. Indeed, the latter's music was often heard at the Great Room that season; Ogle played his 'Harpsichord Concerto' on 4 January 1752, and concertos by him rounded off the thirteenth, fourteenth and eighteenth concerts.[26] If Ogle

---

21 See the advertisement in the *Public Advertiser* for their concert at Hickford's Great Room on 18 February 1766. C. F. Pohl, *Mozart und Haydn in London*. 2 vols. (Wien: Carl Gerold's Sohn, 1867), 2:374, makes brief reference to the Collas' visits to London in 1753 and 1766.
22 See RISM ID nos. 211011814-211011819 and *NGD*, 6:93.
23 TNA: C 11/804/26.
24 TNA: ASSI 45/21/4/54 and 45/21/4/55A; *Extracts from the records of the merchant adventurers of Newcastle Upon Tyne*, ed. J. R. Boyle and F. W. Dendy. 2 vols. Publications of the Surtees Society 93 and 101 (1895–99), 2:258.
25 *General Advertiser* 11 March 1751.
26 *General Advertiser* for 7 and 14 March, and 11 April 1752.

Illustration App. 2.1 Pier Leone Ghezzi, 'Domenico con Suo Fratello Bresciani'. Typ 720.66.423, Houghton Library, Harvard University.

Engraving from *Raccolta de' vari disegni* (1766).

had hoped to rebuild his reputation for fiscal probity using the profits from this subscription series, he was to be disappointed; his substantial freehold estate in the north east was sold to the highest bidder in December 1751, and the capital raised was divided among his creditors at London's Guildhall on 2 April following.[27] As a practicing musician his name thereafter disappears

---

27 *London Gazette* 26–30 November 1751, and 25–29 February 1752.

116 *Appendix 2*

from the newspapers, although the concert venue in Dean Street was still referred to as 'Mr Ogle's' as late as the spring of 1754. He was committed to the King's Bench Prison on 21 June 1753 and his certificate of bankruptcy was issued on 25 August following;[28] Mr Justice Wright discharged him from prison on 10 November, and eight months later his creditors made a second dividend of his effects, at which point he probably resolved to seek his fortune on the other side of the Atlantic.[29] Advertisements such as the following, which were occasionally placed in the London papers with a view to recruiting volunteers to emigrate to the colonies, may have encouraged him to do so (see Illustration App. 2.2):

> *Wanted directly for the Weſt-Indies, North America, &c.*
> TWO regular Clergymen, a Muſician, two Dancing-Maſters, a Man that underſtands acting upon the Stage in a Playhouſe, and two young Ladies that underſtand the ſame in a Playhouſe; alſo two Men that underſtand blowing the French Horn, and other Muſick; alſo a Woman Houſekeeper that can make a grand Appearance, two Ladies Maids that can make a genteel Appearance, that underſtand playing on the Harpſichord and Spinnet, two young Ladies that can teach French, and two Women Cooks that can make a genteel Appearance; alſo two Maſons, two Houſe-Carpenters and Joyners, four Wheelwrights, three Millwrights, four Shipwrights, two Plumbers and Glaziers, two Copperſmiths, two Coopers, and two Blackſmiths and Farriers. Any of the above that is qualified ſhall have the beſt Encouragement that ever was given. Alſo ſeveral Hundreds of handicraft Trades and Huſbandmen wanted as Servants; alſo Lads and young Women may go with their Friends Conſent, to any of his Majeſty's Plantations abroad. Apply to Criſp's Office at the Lamb and Crown in Threadneedle-Street, near the South-Sea-Houſe, London.

Illustration App. 2.2 Advertisement for personnel to emigrate to the Americas. Courtesy of the British Library.

Daily Advertiser 9 January 1754.

Cuthbert probably left England in the autumn of 1754, for in the following December his wife advertised for suitable help in running the concert venue:

> Mr Ogle, formerly Manager of the above Concert Room, having given up and entirely quitted that Affair, and gone abroad upon some advantageous Offers to the West-Indies, a proper Person is wanted as

---

28 TNA: PRIS 4/2 (King's Bench Commitment Book 1747–58): no. 1264; *London Gazette* 31 July–4 August 1753.
29 *London Gazette* 2–6 July 1754.

an Assistant in the Management of the Assembly, &c. A Person that understands Musick will be the most agreeable.[30]

Cuthbert arrived in Williamsburg, Virginia, early in 1755, and advertised his services as a teacher of the organ, harpsichord and spinet, but he soon fell ill and died there on 23 April.[31] An inventory of his music and instruments taken at the time shows that he owned a copy of James Nares's *Eight setts of lessons for the harpsichord* (1747), which almost certainly identifies him as the 'Mr Ogle, of Newcastle' who is listed among the subscribers to that publication.[32] In August 1755 Mrs Ogle, wishing to retire from concert management on account of her husband's death, sought to rent out, or dispose of, the Great Room, but it was several years before she could achieve that objective.[33] In the meantime she was forced to diversify, and the space was used as a meeting room, a school for dancing and a ballroom, as well as a concert venue.[34] On 17 December 1759, Dr Johnson wrote to Mrs Elizabeth Montagu requesting her favour on behalf of 'Mrs. Ogle, who kept the musick-room in Soho Square, a woman who struggles with great industry for the support of eight children, [and who] hopes by a Benefit Concert to see herself free from a few debts, which she cannot otherwise discharge'.[35] A newspaper advertisement shows that by June 1761 the tenancy had been taken over by the violinist and concert promoter Giuseppe Passerini. It also provides interesting information about the size of the property and the dimensions of the hall: 'the Length (including the Orchestra) is about 70 Feet, the Breadth 33 Feet and a half, and the Height [*sic*] 24 Feet'.[36] No further information regarding Mrs Ogle's whereabouts after this date has come to light.

30 *Public Advertiser* 19 December 1754.
31 John W. Molnar, 'A collection of music in colonial Virginia: The Ogle inventory', *The Musical Quarterly* 49/2 (April 1963), 150–62.
32 See Janet K. Page, 'The hautboy in London's musical life, 1730–1770', *Early Music* 16/3 (August 1988), 359–71, at 368; and Margaret Seares, 'The composer and the subscriber: A case study from the 18th century', *Early Music* 39/1 (February 2011), 65–78, at 74.
33 *Public Advertiser* 13 August 1755; ibid., 24 October 1757; ibid., 13 June 1761.
34 By 1769 it appears to have been an auction room run by a Mr Blythe.
35 *The letters of Samuel Johnson*, ed. R. W. Chapman. 3 vols. (Oxford: Clarendon Press, 1952), 1:125.
36 *Whitehall Evening Post or London Intelligencer* 4–6 June 1761. The Dean Street venue was bigger than Hickford's, which measured 'about fifty feet long, thirty feet wide and twenty-two feet high'; see Robert Elkin, *The Old Concert Rooms of London* (London: Edward Arnold, 1955), 44. An advertisement for a benefit performance of Handel's *Acis and Galatea* on 1 April 1758 informed the public that: 'A greater Number of Tickets being disposed of than Mr. Hickford's Room can contain, makes it necessary to remove the Performance to Dean-street, where Tickets delivered out for Mr. Hickford's for this Day will be taken' (*Public Advertiser* 31 March 1758).

Winch, Christopher (fl. c.1725–61)

The 'Mr Winch' to whom Giardini owed money in April 1755 was almost certainly the Christopher Winch who is listed among the original subscribers to the Royal Society of Musicians on 28 August 1739, and who was still a member in 1755.[37] A foreign horn-player active in London from the mid-1720s, Winch may have been the author of *The compleat tutor for the French horn* – the first known individual method published for the instrument.[38] In March 1733 he played for John Frederick Lampe in Fielding's musical farce *The mock doctor* at the Little Theatre in the Haymarket, and in the following May he earned 7s 6d a night as a member of the band for *The opera of operas*.[39] He is also recorded as participating in concerts at Stationers' Hall (March 1735), Drury Lane (May 1736), and the Devil Tavern at Temple Bar (May 1738). During the early years of the next decade Winch spent some time in Ireland. In October 1741 the *Dublin News-Letter* reported that on the 22nd instant 'a Concerto on the French Horn by the celebrated Mr Winch, who has perform'd several years in Mr Handel's Operas and Oratorios' would be heard between the acts of the play at Smock Alley theatre; and at the same venue on 27 February following, Winch had a benefit in the course of which he played several concertos of his own composition.[40] By the middle of the decade he was back in London, taking part in musical events at the Devil Tavern in March 1745 and at the Castle in Pater Noster Row a year later. Winch's first wife died in the parish of St Anne Soho in 1747, and later that year he married Frances Tabart, widow, by licence at St Mary's Putney. He appears to have taken his final bow as a soloist in Master Jonathan Snow's benefit at the Little Haymarket on 2 April 1750, though he may have continued to play in orchestras. Tickets for that concert were available from various outlets, including 'Mr. Winch's at the Turk's Head

---

37 Betty Matthews, *The Royal Society of Musicians of Great Britain: List of Members 1738–1984* (London: Royal Society of Musicians, 1985), 159 and 184. His name is variously spelled 'Winsch', 'Wynch', or 'Wench' in the newspapers.

38 *The compleat tutor for the French horn* (London: J. Simpson, c.1745; 2nd edn, Peter Thompson, c.1765). Jennifer Beakes suggests that Winch may have been the horn player 'Mr Witch', whom John Grano mentions twice in diary entries for August 1729; see her *The horn parts in Handel's operas and oratorios and the horn players who performed in these works*. (DMA thesis, City University of New York, 2007), 457–58; and *Handel's trumpeter: The diary of John Grano*, ed. J. Ginger (New York: Pendragon Press, 1998), 303 and 305. The earliest reference to Winch dates from 19 Nov 1726, when he married Mary Ferry at St Mary Magdalene, Old Fish Street, London.

39 See Milhous and Hume, 'J. F. Lampe and English Opera', 526.

40 Brian Boydell, *A Dublin musical calendar 1700–1760*. (Dublin: Irish Academic Press, 1988), 74 and 78.

[on] the Corner of Greek-Street, Soho'. During the ten years he was the tavern's landlord it served as a ticket agency, a rehearsal space, and a meeting place for learned societies; and from February 1753 the Governors of the Society of Musicians held their monthly meetings there, possibly at his instigation.[41] It is difficult to say whether the £10 9s 6d in which Giardini was indebted to Winch arose from unpaid dues owed to the latter as an orchestral musician or from the wine with which he supplied Giardini as a vintner. In the late 1750s Winch sought to circumvent the legal disabilities attached to his status as an alien living in Great Britain by applying for denization; this was granted by letters patent on 15 February 1759, and enabled him lawfully to 'Acquire Receive Take Have Hold Purchase and Possess Lands Tenements Rents Revenues and Services and all other Hereditaments whatsoever within Our said Kingdom ... And Give Sell Alienate and Bequeath the same to any Person or Persons as [he] shall think fit'.[42] About this time he moved out of Greek Street and opened a public house at No. 9 Gerrard Street, retaining the name of his former establishment.[43] In late November 1760 'Christopher Winch of the parish of Saint Ann Westm*inste*ʳ Vintner' made his will, leaving everything to his wife Frances.[44] Some six months later the *London Evening Post* carried the following notice: 'Tuesday [2 June] died of a Paralytic Disorder, Mr. Christopher Winch, Master of the Turk's Head Tavern in Gerrard-street, Soho'.[45] The day of his death coincided with a rehearsal at the Turk's Head of 'the ode for his Majesty's birthday, composed by William Whitehead, Esq. and set to music by Dr. Boyce, ... by the Gentlemen of his Majesty's Chapel Royal, and the King's band of music, &c'.[46] Winch's burial is recorded in the St Anne's registers on 6 June.

---

41 *Public Advertiser* 27 January 1753.
42 William A. Shaw, *Letters of denization and acts of naturalization for aliens in England and Ireland 1701–1800*. Publications of the Huguenot Society of London 27 (1923), 160; C 66/3664: patent 23.
43 *Survey of London 33–34: The Parish of St Anne Soho*, gen. ed. F. H. W. Sheppard (London: Athlone Press, 1966), 33:171, 34:388.
44 TNA: PCC Wills; PROB 11/866/111.
45 See issue dated 2–4 June 1761.
46 *Public Ledger or The Daily Register of Commerce and Intelligence* 2 June 1761.

Index

A B C Dario Musico 13n19, 21
Abel, Carl Friedrich 83n13, 94
academies 11, 15
accompanied keyboard sonata 38
Alberti, Domenico 82
Albinoni, Tomaso Giovanni 82
Alessandro nell'Indie (pasticcio) 65
'An act ... for regulating places of publick entertainment' (25 Geo. II, c. 36) 44
Arne, Thomas Augustus 72; *Abel* 61; *Alfred* 61; *Love in a village* 17
Atfield, John 31
Avison, Charles 17, 38, 48, 114; opinion of Giardini 12

Bach, Johann Christian 94, 100, 111
Bach/Abel concerts 108n28
Baretti, Giuseppe 110n5
Bartolozzi, Francesco 89
Bath 13–14, 19, 96, 110
Baumgarten, Samuel 45
Beard, John 113
Bedford, 4th Duke of 111
Beneke, Mr 14
Benson, Robert Lord Bingley 14; Bramham Park 15–16, 18; London residence 15
Berlin 9
Besozzi, Alessandro 27, 85, 103, 107n17
Bingley, Lady *see* Lane, Harriet
blue paper 34, 102
Bottarelli, Giovanni Gualberto 112
Bowes, George and Mary 17–19

Boyce, William 72, 119
Bremner, Robert 29
Brescia 113
Bristol 14
Brown, Abraham 12
Burney, Charles 3; on Giardini's acceptance into fashionable society 51; on Giardini and Mingotti's opera season 64–5; on Giardini's impact on musical taste 82–3; on Harriet Lane's patronage of Giardini 15; opinion of Giardini 11–12, 21, 100–1
Burrows, Donald 24

Cahusac, Thomas 28
Call, Thomas 82n11
Campioni, Carlo Antonio 111
Carbonelli, Giovanni Stefano 13n16
castrati 15–16
Cattanei, Signor 113
Cervetto, Ciacobbe 49n36
Chabran, Charles (Carlo Giuseppe Valentino Chiabrano) 53, 102, 106n7, 109–11, 113; concert series with Giardini 57–60, 86, 91–2, 99, 110; death 60, 111; his initial support from Giardini 49, 89; his rivalry with Giardini 49–50, 53, 110; Op. 1 *Six sonates à violon seul et basse continüe* 85, 109; as orchestral leader 49, 57
Chabran/Chiabrano, Signora 58, 109–10
Chancery, Court of 28, 114; Master of the Rolls 28

122 *Index*

Chapel Royal 24
Chiabrano, Giovanni Nicola 109
Ciampi/Chiampi, Vincenzo 72, 85, 103, 111–12; *Didone* 112; *La famiglia de' Bertholdi* 112
Cipriani, Giovanni Battista 89
clandestine marriages 23n48, 25
Cobb, Thomas 74n14
colascione and *colascioncino/ colasciontino* 113–15
Colla brothers (Domenico and Giuseppe) 89, 103, 107n23, 110, 113–15
Collet, Richard 12
common law 5, 7, 67, 69
concert programmes 1, 46, 48, 50, 53, 58–60, 83–7
Concert Spirituel 10, 53, 109
Conforto, Nicola: *Antigono* 65
consumerism 1–2
Copyright Act (1710) 40
Corelli, Arcangelo 59, 82
Cowper, Spencer 18
Cox, Hugh 24
Cox, John 22, 24–32, 109–10, 113; as administrator at the Opera 63–6, 76; as advertising agent 89–93; Ann and Lucy (daughters) 30; catalogue 86; as concert administrator 51–2, 54, 56, 59, 61–3, 74–5; as dealer in musical instruments 26; death 32; goods and services sold to Giardini 77–93; at law 3–8, 67–9; lends money to Giardini 68, 99; marries Ann Simpson 25; moves to Kingsland 27, 30; moves to Stanmore 27, 30; as opportunist 99; as publisher 69, 74; purchases Giardini's Op. 3 37–8, 41–3, 69; purchases Giardini's Opp. 1, 2, 4 and Overtures 41–3, 69–70; range of merchandise 26, 29; relationship with Giardini 4, 24, 99–101; Sun insurance policy 26–7
Cox, Thomas 25
Crawford, Peter 64, 76
Crosa, Giovanni Francesco 43, 111
Cumberland, Countess of 110

Cumberland, Duke of 44
Curioni, Rosa 21, 60–1, 87
Curtis, William 29
Cuzzoni, Francesca 10–11

Davies, Miss Marianne 112
Dean, Winton 24
Defoe, Daniel 25n59
Dellavalle, Federico 89–90, 113
Dublin: Smock Alley Theatre 118
Duparc, Elizabeth ('La Francesina') 45
Durham 17–18

Eiffert, Philip 49n36
Ellicott, John and Edward 26–7, 104
entrepreneurialism 2–4, 99
equity 5, 7, 69
Eugene, Prince of Savoy 110
Exchequer, Court of 5–8, 34, 36, 41, 56, 59, 65, 67, 69, 99

Farinelli (Broschi, Carlo) 16
Fawkes, Francis 15
Ferrari, Domenico 27, 105, 108n31; *Six sonatas for a violin and a bass* 86
Festing, Michael Christian 12, 21, 42, 45
Fétis, François-Joseph 10, 109
Fielding, Henry: *The mock doctor* 118
Fischer, Johann Christian 94
Fiske, Roger 10
Fletcher, John: *The Chances* 82
Foote, Samuel: *The Englishman in Paris* 82
Ford, Ann 94
Fourmantel, Catherine 59
Fox Lane, George, later 2nd Lord Bingley 15–16
Fox Lane, Harriet *see* Lane, Harriet
Frasi, Giulia 11n11, 17, 21, 49, 55–6, 89, 104, 107n27, 109–10, 113; concert series with Giardini 60–3, 75, 99
Frederick, Prince of Wales 10, 44, 50; Duchy of Cornwall 10; Princess Dowager of Wales 44
Frederick the Great 9, 114
Froud, Charles 48n31, 49n36

Gainsborough, Thomas 13; portrait of Giardini 94–7
galant style 100
Galli, Caterina 14, 17, 45, 56, 89, 113
Galuppi, Baldassare: *Euristeo* 65; *Penelope* 87; *Ricimero* 61
Gambarini, Elisabetta 110
Garrick, David 96
Garth, John 17–18
Geminiani, Francesco 42, 46, 59, 82, 84, 102, 105, 106n1
Gervasio, Giovanni Battista 81n8
Ghezzi, Pier Leone 114
Giacomazzi, Margarita 112
Giardini, Felice 9–22, 26, 29, 43–5, 74–6, 111, 113, 119; account at Cox's music shop 77–97, 102–5; before coming to England 9–10; concert series with Chabran 57–60, 75, 86, 91–2; concert series with Frasi 60–3, 75; concert series with Ogle 45–9; concert series with Vincent 50–6, 75, 84; at the Concert Spirituel 10; confusion with Tommaso Giordani 17; and Gainsborough in Ipswich 96–7; his royal licence to print 38–42, 69–70; as instrument dealer 13, 81; at law 5–8, 67–9; and the Lock Hospital 24; London début 10–11; marries Vestris 18–21; modern tendencies 2, 36, 48, 82, 84–5; music purchases 82–8; Op. 1 *Sei sonate a violino solo e basso* 22, 33–5, 40–1; Op. 2 *Sei duetti a due violini* 33–5, 40–1; Op. 3 *Sei sonate di cembalo con violino o flauto traverso* 18, 26, 35–8, 41–2, 48, 74; Op. 4 *Sei arie* 38, 40; Op. 6 *XII Sonates à violon seul avec la basse* 41; Op 15 *Six concertos in seven parts* 41; Op. 18 *Six trios for the guittar, violin and pianoforte (or harp, violin and violoncello*) 82; as opera impresario 63–6, 99; as opportunist 3, 99; and orchestral discipline 21; as orchestral leader 9, 45, 47, 61, 100, 113; Overtures 2, 10, 40–3, 67, 69–74, 99–100, 105; owns Gainsborough's 'Figures before a Cottage' 96; promissory notes 68–9; and receives discounts from Cox 38, 80, 86–7; rivalry with Chabran 49–50, 110; *Rosmira* 65–6; self-publishing 33–4; as soloist 10–11, 46–8, 84; sponsors Italian musicians 49, 88–9, 99, 109; as teacher 11–13, 80–2, 100; tours Germany 9; tours north-east England 14–21; violin alterations 78–9; violin pupils 12–13, 18, 78; violin strings 26, 80, 86, 102–5; as virtuoso 2, 12–13, 50, 100; *VI Trii per cetra, violino e basso* 82
Gibbs, Joseph 97
Gibside, Gateshead 17–18
Giulini, Conte Giorgio 48
Gladwin, Thomas 38
Grafton, Duke of 64
Granom, Lewis Christian Austin 27–8, 44; *XII New songs and ballads* Op. 4 28
Greene, Maurice 72
Grumeant/Gramiant, John 71–2
Guadagni, Gaetano 49
guittar 81–2, 104–5

Hallifax, Charles: *Familiar letters on various subjects* 84n16
Hamilton, Sir William: as pupil of Giardini 12
Handel, George Frideric 14–15, 51, 59–60, 82, 118; *The Choice of Hercules* 61; *Joseph and his brethren* 61; *Judas Maccabaeus* 61; *L'Allegro, il Pensoroso ed il Moderato* 60n66, 107n27; royal licence 42; *Samson* 61; *Theodora* 61
Hare family 22, 26n64, 28, 106n1
Harris, Elizabeth 63n74
Harris, Thomas 51
Hasse, Johann Adolf: *Il re pastore* 65–6; *I pellegrini* 24; *Ipermestra* 87; *Penelope* 87
Hay/Hey/Hays, Richard: as pupil of Giardini 12–13, 18
Heidegger, Johann Jakob 15
Heinrich, Prince of Prussia 34

124 *Index*

Hickford, John 44
Hickford's Room 11, 43–4, 112, 114n21; entertainment licence 44
Hintz, John Frederick 81–2
Hogarth, William: *Marriage à la mode* 16
Holman, Peter 80
Hugford, James 44, 46

Jackson, John 16
Jackson, William 38
Johnson, Dr Samuel 117
Johnson, John 85, 112
Jommelli, Niccolò: *Demofoonte* 73, 93

King's Bench, Court of 5–7, 63, 67–8, 112; King's Bench Prison 116
Knerler, Mr 13n16

Lalauze, Charles 63
Lampe, John Frederick 118
Lampugnani, Giovanni Battista 85, 103, 107n16; *Ipermestra* 87; *Siroe, Rè di Persia* 87–8, 93
Lane, Harriet 14–20, 63–4, 67; as dedicatee of Giardini's overtures 74; enthusiasm for Italian music 16; love of horse-racing 16; as patron of Giardini 14–15, 17, 50; 'On a Raptur'd Lady' 15
Lane, John 67
Lane, Robert 15n25
Lanesborough, Viscount 15
Lanzetti, Salvatore 58–9
Leoni/Leoné, Gabriele 81n8
Linley family 94
London: Birchin Lane, Cornhill 22; Bow Church, Cheapside 27; Brewer Street, St James's 6, 11, 43–4; the Castle Tavern, Pater Noster Row 118; Covent Garden (Theatre Royal) 1, 61, 107n27, 112; the Devil Tavern, Temple Bar 118; Drury Lane (Theatre Royal) 1, 61, 118; Fleet prison 23, 63n73; Frith Street, Soho 45; Gerrard Street, Soho 107n27, 119; Great Room, Dean Street, Soho 21, 43–7, 49–61, 63, 86–92, 110, 112, 114, 117; Greek Street, Soho 112; heating music venues 46, 88; Hickford's Room 11, 43–4, 112, 113; King's Arms Concert 83, 110; Kingsland, Hackney 27, 30, 32; King's Theatre, Haymarket 1, 43–4, 59–61, 63–6, 87, 112; Lock Hospital 24; Marylebone 106n8; Mr Philidor's Concert 110; musical life 1–3; musicians' charity concerts 61, 66n79, 110; New or 'Little' Theatre, Haymarket 10–11, 54, 89, 109, 113, 118; opera 1, 3, 14, 43–6, 50, 59–61, 63–6, 69, 74, 76, 87, 93, 99–101, 105; Ranelagh 27, 109, 113; Royal Exchange 22, 25–6; 'the season' 14; St Anne Soho 118–19; Stationers' Hall 118; St Bartholomew Exchange 23, 30; St Bartholomew the Great, West Smithfield 22; St George's Chapel, Mayfair 25; St Leonard's Shoreditch 23; St Martin's Street 109; St Mary's Putney 118; St Mary Stoke Newington 23; St Michael Queenhithe 23; St Michael's Alley, Cornhill 25; St Pancras cemetery 111; subscription concerts 43–63; Sweeting's/Swithin's Alley 22–3, 25–6, 29; Vauxhall Gardens 1, 29; Windmill Street 44
Lunéville 22

Macklin, Maria 82
Madan, Rev. Martin 100n1
Mahoon, Joseph 102, 106n8
mandoline/manderlean 81, 105
Manfredini, Giuseppe Maria 44
Marella, Giovanni Battista 82
Marine Society 66
Marlborough, 1st Duke of 110
Marlborough, 3rd Duke of 64
Marzi, Pasqualino di 82
Mattei, Colomba 87
McVeigh, Simon 21–2, 84–5
Merchi, Giacomo and Giuseppe Bernardo 113n15
Milan 9, 48
Miller, John 45, 49n36, 56, 58n62, 89
Mingotti, Regina 21, 61, 63–4, 73–4, 76, 87–8, 93
Mondonville, Jean-Joseph Cassanéa de 103, 107n15; *Pièces de clavecin en*

sonates avec accompagnement de violon Op. 3 38, 85
Montagu, Elizabeth 117
Morigi, Angelo 85, 103, 107n18
Mortimer, Thomas: *Universal Director* 80, 82
music plates 29, 33–4, 37, 42, 70–2, 102

Naples 9
Nardini, Pietro 108n31
Nares, George 67
Nares, James 14, 18, 67, 117
Newcastle upon Tyne 17, 114, 117
Noferi, Giovanni Battista 18n35, 82

Oesterreich, Matthias 114
Ogle, Cuthbert 57, 84, 99, 115–17; concert series 45–50; emigrates to Williamsburg, Virginia 116–17; as harpsichordist 45, 47–8, 115; inventory of personal effects 117; success of concert series 48–9
Ogle, Mrs Mary: as manager of the Great Room, Dean Street 21, 45, 54–6, 62, 106, 108n38, 111, 114–17
Onofrio, Signor 18
opportunism 2–3, 99
O'Reilly, Robert Bray 64
Oswald, James 28, 82

Paladini, Giuseppe Pietro 9
Palma, Signor 44
Paris 10, 21–2, 27, 49, 53, 74n15, 85, 100, 109
Parke, William Thomas 13, 94
Parma, Duke of 107n18
Pasquali, Francis 71–2
Pasquali, Niccolo 47, 72
Pasqualino/Pasqualini, Peter 27, 45, 46, 56, 61, 89, 109
Passerini, Giuseppe and Christina 59–60, 117; 'Spiritual Concerts' 57
Patoni, Giovanna Battista 27
patronage 1, 16–17, 43
Penvold, James 105, 108n34
Phillips, John 71
Piedmont school of violin-playing 12
Pinto, Thomas 21
piracy 27–8, 40, 100

Plà brothers 57–9
Provok'd Wife, The (John Vanbrugh) 17

Quantz, Johann Joachim 9

Rameau, Jean-Philippe 48, 105, 108n32; *Pièces de clavecin en concert* 38, 86
Ranieri, Nicola 112
repertoire *see* concert programmes
Resta, Natale 111
Reynolds, Sir Joshua 94
Ricciarelli, Giuseppe 21, 87, 93
Robinson, Miss 44
Rome 9
Royal Academy of Music 14, 43
royal licences 27–8, 38–43, 69
Royal Society of Musicians 118–19
Ruckholt House, Essex 107n19
Russell, Lady Caroline 111

Sackville family (Dukes of Dorset) 94–6
Saint-Germain, Comte de 43
Sammartini, Giovanni Battista 9, 11, 48, 72–3, 86, 103–4
Sammartini, Giuseppe 10, 72, 85
Scarborough 14
Scarlatti, Domenico 82
Schabran, Mr. *see* Chabran, Charles (Carlo Giuseppe Valentino Chiabrano)
Schedules 6–7; Schedule A1 102–8; Schedule A2 34, 41, 81; Schedule B1 7, 56, 75; Schedule B2 7, 65–6
Senesino (Bernardi, Francesco) 16
Sheward, Miss 45, 49, 110
Shield, William 13
Simpson, John and Anne (née Briscoe) 22–4
Simpson's Music Shop 26, 28–9, 33, 58, 60, 100, 109
Small, John 40n13
Snow, Jonathan 118
Somis, Giovanni Battista 9, 109
Stanisław I, King of Poland 22
Stanmore, Middlesex 27, 30
Storace family 112

tanbūr 113
Tartini, Giuseppe 83–4, 102–3, 106n2

Index

Tessarini, Carlo 83, 85–6, 103, 107n19; *Il piacer delle dame* 27
Thicknesse, Philip 95
Thompson family: Charles and Samuel 29; Peter and Robert 28
Thorowgood, Henry 29
ticket prices 45, 49, 52–3, 57–60
Tunbridge Wells 19
Turin 9, 109; Teatro Regio 109
Turner, Elizabeth 49
Turpin de Crissé, Comte Lancelot 34

Unwin, James 13
Ursillo, Fabio 27

Vachon, Pierre 109
Vanneschi, Francesco 60, 63, 88n28, 110n5
Venier, Jean Baptiste 10
Veracini, Francesco Maria 83
Vestris, Maria Caterina Violante 17–21, 52–6, 58, 90–2, 113; marries Giardini 18–20

Vincent, Thomas junior 45, 48, 60, 84, 89, 109; concert series with Giardini 50–6, 85, 99
Vivaldi, Antonio 82

Walsh, John 29, 38, 43, 48, 85–8, 93, 111–12; catalogue 84, 86
Waylett, Henry 28
Wearman, Miss *31*
Weber, William 2–3, 100
Welcker, Peter 111
Whitaker, Maurice Philips 24, 28–9
Whitehead, William 119
Wilkinson, Tate 16
Williamsburg, Virginia 117
Winch, Christopher 118–19; *The compleat tutor for the French horn* 118
Woodcock, Robert 84, 102, 106n3
Worgan, John 42

York 14–21, 60; Assembly Rooms, Blake Street 14; August Race week 14; summer Assize week 14

For Product Safety Concerns and Information please contact our EU
representative GPSR@taylorandfrancis.com
Taylor & Francis Verlag GmbH, Kaufingerstraße 24, 80331 München, Germany

www.ingramcontent.com/pod-product-compliance
Lightning Source LLC
Chambersburg PA
CBHW051753230426
43670CB00012B/2262